the
SWORD
& the
SPIRIT

A 40-Day
Morning & Evening
Devotional

JOHN GRECO

BroadStreet
PUBLISHING

BroadStreet Publishing® Group, LLC
Savage, Minnesota, USA
BroadStreetPublishing.com

The Sword and the Spirit: A 40-Day Morning and Evening Devotional
Copyright © 2023 John Greco

9781424565641 (faux leather)
9781424565658 (ebook)

Stock or custom editions of BroadStreet Publishing titles may be purchased in bulk for educational, business, ministry, fundraising, or sales promotional use. For information, please email orders@broadstreetpublishing.com.

Cover and interior by Garborg Design Works | garborgdesign.com

Printed in China

23 24 25 26 27 5 4 3 2 1

For Uncle Tom and Aunt Roe.

I have watched you wield the Sword and walk by the
Spirit my entire life, and I am grateful for you both.

A Note to the Reader

This book was written primarily for believers—for men and women who love Jesus and have made a commitment to follow him. In fact, much of what is written in these pages will only carry weight in your life if you have been born again. That said, if you happen to be a seeker or a skeptic or someone who walked away from God some years ago, my hope is that these readings will inspire you to seek the Lord and discover what you've been missing.

Concerning the Sword

In Scripture, when "the word of God," "the word of the Lord," or "the word of the LORD" is used, one of several concepts may be in view: God's direct speech (Psalm 33:6); his messages spoken by his prophets (Isaiah 1:10); his commandments (Deuteronomy 5:5); his judgments (Hebrews 4:12); his appearances in human form (Jeremiah 1:4–9); the Son of God (John 1:1–2, 14); the gospel message (Acts 8:25); and the written Word, both the Old and New Testaments (2 Timothy 4:2). For this reason, I've capitalized *word* only when using it as a synonym for Scripture or the Son.

While this book deals primarily with the Bible and its place in our lives, there are times when we will explore other aspects of the word of God. It's important to understand and take note of the distinctions, but drawing hard lines may not always be worthwhile. That's because each meaning is related to all the others, and every nuance brings God's heart to bear. And that's really what we're after: God's heart.

CONCERNING THE SPIRIT

Some believers (and you may be included among them) hold that the sign gifts of the Holy Spirit, including miracles, healings, tongues, and prophecy, ceased after the apostles died. However, the Bible never gives any indication the gifts poured out on the New Testament church were given only for a limited time. In fact, there are passages that appear to teach just the opposite. (See, for example, 1 Corinthians 13:8–12.) It is my conviction that we must allow Scripture to inform our experiences rather than allow our experiences to color our reading of Scripture. Therefore, this book celebrates all the gifts of the Holy Spirit.

Concerning the Order of Readings

Though the title of this book, *The Sword and the Spirit*, might suggest that readings about the Sword would come before the readings about the Spirit each day, the opposite is true. My hope is that, each morning, you'll read and be reminded to walk in step with the Holy Spirit throughout your day, and then each evening, as the busyness of life winds down, you'll be refreshed by the unchanging truth of God's Word.

I believe that the church will live up to its calling in our day when, and only when, believers across the spectrum of denominations and traditions embrace the entirety of the Word and the fullness of the Spirit. That's the heart behind this little book. I pray it is an encouragement to you in your daily walk with Jesus.

FREE TO BE YOU

Now the Lord is the Spirit,
and where the Spirit of the Lord is,
there is freedom.

2 CORINTHIANS 3:17

These days, freedom can seem just out of reach. Most of us spend the lion's share of our minutes and our hours doing the things we *need* to do rather than the things we'd *like* to do. Jobs and chores and loved ones demand our attention. To step away and enjoy a time of true refreshment is a luxury that often feels just too pricey. And yet, the Bible describes the normal Christian life as one of glorious freedom.

To know Jesus is to have the Holy Spirit living inside. That means he is here with us all the time, whether we're racing to check off the next item on our to-do list or collapsing into bed at night. So where is this freedom the Spirit is supposed to bring with him? Where is the relief we were promised?

True freedom, according to the Bible, goes far beyond having lots of choices and plenty of free time. It's more than the pursuit of happiness or having money in the bank. The sweet freedom the Holy Spirit brings to us is the freedom to come home to ourselves, to be the people God created us to be.

Back in Eden, God created the first man and woman to be part of his family. Quite literally, they were made for him—to know him, love him, and be loved by him. In that, there was total and complete freedom. That's not to say there wasn't work to do (see Genesis 2:15). Rather, the freedom of Eden was peace and joy and a heart filled with worship.

When we lost paradise, we lost this freedom. No one has been able to live in true freedom since. No one except Jesus. He came to show us the freedom that was once our birthright. Not only that, he came to restore it (John 8:36). On the cross, he took the punishment for our sins so we could draw near to God. Then he gave us the Holy Spirit to transform our hearts and minds so we can be people of Eden once again, people who look a lot like Jesus.

Through the Spirit at work in your life, you "are being transformed into his image with ever-increasing glory" (2 Corinthians 3:18). It's happening one day at a time, little by little, so that you may know the freedom you were meant to walk in.

Father, tune my heart and mind to the promptings of your Spirit so I can experience the freedom I was made for.

LIGHT IN THE DARKNESS

Your word is a lamp for my feet,
a light on my path.
PSALM 119:105

There's a reason many children are afraid of the dark. Darkness is the realm of the unknown, where our sense of sight is blunted and each step carries risk. There's no telling what may be lurking just beyond our gait.

Of course, everyone grows up. Some of us shed our fear of the dark because we imagine there's nothing to be afraid of. Others no longer fear because they've come to see the darkness as a friend who promises to keep all their secrets (John 3:19). They'd rather hide from the light than walk in it.

But there's no hiding from God. He sees everything that happens in the darkness. He views all the stumbles and the falls, the tears and the heartaches. He knows every misstep and every regret. His heart is to rescue people from the darkness, to heal them and bring them into his kingdom (Colossians 1:13). That is why he sent Jesus, who is himself the Light that shatters the night (John 1:5). It's also why he gave us his Word.

With so many people living in darkness all around us, this world is a shadowland, even for those who know the Lord. The Bible is, for us, the brightest of flashlights to shine on our path. When we read, our eyes are opened to the truth, and the lies of the devil fall flat. When we study, we learn to see through the empty philosophies of this world so that their appeals can no longer hold us captive. And when we take hold of the Bible's promises, our gaze is lifted up out of this dark valley toward the heavens, where our hope is kept.

Of course, a lamp must be turned on to be effective. In the same way, we must take up God's Word daily if we are going to make our way through this dark world. Though a flashlight may grow dim from use, the light of God's Word only grows brighter as we walk in it.

You have not been left to wander in the night. The Lord has given you a mighty torch to dispel the darkness. Are you confused? Go to his Word. Afraid? Take comfort in his precious promises. Searching for answers to life's most important questions? Invest your time in the book that has them.

God lives in the purest, sweetest light there is, and you've been invited to follow him there (Psalm 89:15). Take up and read!

Lord, make your light shine through me as your Word illuminates the path you've set before me.

NEVER ALONE AGAIN

"I will not leave you as orphans;
I will come to you."

JOHN 14:18

They were there when he opened the eyes of the blind, unstopped the ears of the deaf, and restored the strength of the paralyzed. They'd seen him silence storms, command demons, and raise up the dead. His parables and teachings, not easily forgotten, filled their minds and their hearts. The disciples were convinced Jesus of Nazareth was the Messiah whom God had promised his people, the King who would reign in Jerusalem forever.

But then, Jesus seemed to go off script. He started talking about leaving, about returning to the Father, about preparing rooms for them in the Father's house (vv. 1–4). It didn't make sense. It didn't fit with their understanding of the Scriptures or keep time with the hope beating in their chests. They didn't want to be left alone again, not after all they'd seen and heard. They wanted more of Jesus, not less.

Jesus knew their hearts, and he knows ours. This desire for greater intimacy with him, for more eternal truth, for more kingdom goodness is nothing to be brushed aside; it's in our DNA, given to us when God breathed life into Adam.

Though his friends didn't understand how it could be possible, Jesus promised to be a greater presence in their lives through the gift of the Holy Spirit than he had been when he walked and talked with them during his earthly ministry. He told them, "On that day you will realize that I am in my Father, and you are in me, and I am in you" (v. 20).

The Father, the Son, and the Holy Spirit enjoy perfect fellowship, and through the Spirit in our lives, we can enter in. We have been invited to partake of the love they share, to be at home in their presence (vv. 21, 23), to enjoy the intimacy we were created for.

How is this connection, this abiding, maintained and enjoyed? The same way it is with any relationship: through love (15:10). God's love, of course, is not something that can be earned. Rather, as you obey the commands of Jesus and chase after his heart, you are choosing to rest in his great love for you—to let it wash over you and cleanse you.

There is no greater joy in the universe than knowing Jesus. Because he has given you his Holy Spirit, he is closer to you than your own skin. Rest in his love.

Jesus, I want to know more of you. May my life be defined by the experience of your presence.

BREATH OF HEAVEN

All Scripture is God-breathed
and is useful for teaching, rebuking,
correcting and training in righteousness.
2 TIMOTHY 3:16

When you stop to think about it, it's incredible. Unthinkable, really. When we were trapped in a dungeon of our own making, God saw fit to bend low and pass a note through the prison bars. He used words we could understand, wrapped in human experience and the universal language of story, to show us the way to freedom.

This "note" is the Bible, the only book in the world that was breathed out by God. That means it's the only book that holds divine authority. We are meant to take the words of Scripture with all the weight of heaven. We would be fools to brush aside what we don't like, to simply disregard what doesn't line up with our own way of thinking in the moment (Proverbs 1:7). And yet, sadly, that's what many people do when they crack open their Bibles. To use our prison analogy, it's like opening up the note we've been given to discover it's a signed and sealed pardon from the governor—and then proceeding to use it as toilet paper.

Scripture shows us the way to salvation (2 Timothy 3:15), but it also shapes us into people who more perfectly reflect the image of God with our lives (Romans 12:1–2). In short, God breathed out his Word so we could breathe it in, each and every day, and by breathing in the air of heaven, we might live as heavenly men and women here on earth.

A person could spend ten lifetimes studying Scripture, and it would still not be enough time to explore all of the divine mysteries contained in God's Word. And yet, the through line of the Bible—God's great love for sinners—is simple enough for a small child to grasp. At times, Scripture peels back the veil between heaven and earth, revealing eternal secrets otherwise unknowable. At others, it delivers insight into the human soul, allowing us to see the depths of our great need under the curse of sin. But mostly, the Bible is God's story, and his beautiful heart can be seen on every page.

Spend time soaking in the Scriptures, and you'll begin to taste a bit of heaven on your tongue (Psalm 34:8). God is good, and his ways lead to love and joy and the true *shalom* of the kingdom—the perfect peace and wholeness that is your inheritance as a child of the King.

Father, reveal your heart to me as I read your Word so I might fall more deeply in love with you.

THE DRY BONES PRAISE

> *"'I will put my Spirit in you
> and you will live.'"*
>
> EZEKIEL 37:14

What does it take to bring a person back from the dead? It's not enough to jumpstart the synapses in the brain so they fire and snap once again, nor is it sufficient to wake the silent heart so that it begins pumping blood through coarse and dried arteries. It isn't simply a matter of inflating lungs and reanimating cells either. To make a dead soul alive, it needs the Spirit of God.

The prophet Ezekiel saw this process unfold before his eyes when, in a vision, God brought him out into the middle of a morbid valley filled with dry bones. The people of Israel were like those bones— beyond dead with no hope of restoration (v. 11). The citizens of the Northern Kingdom had been taken captive by the Assyrians and spread far and wide, in large measure becoming indistinguishable from their pagan neighbors. More than a century later, the people in the south were taken into Babylon. The nation was no more, Jerusalem was toppled, and the temple of God lay in rubble. Worse than that, this calamity was not simply the result of unfolding world events; it was caused by the stubborn, sinful hearts of the people (Deuteronomy 28:36; Jeremiah 16:12–13).

God commanded Ezekiel to prophesy, and the bones he saw rattled and clacked into place. Tendons and muscle and skin soon overtook them. Again, Ezekiel prophesied, and the four winds came and filled those bodies with the breath of life. The vision was a promise to Ezekiel. God would bring the dead nation of Israel back to life. The people would be numerous and mighty. And the wind that would fill his people would be the very Spirit of God (Ezekiel 37:14).

As Jesus put it, "The Spirit gives life; the flesh counts for nothing" (John 6:63). We were once "dead in [our] transgressions and sins" (Ephesians 2:1), but then God came and breathed new life into us. We have been born again, made new, and transferred from the realm of darkness to the kingdom of light by the Holy Spirit (Colossians 1:13).

Never forget that you are a walking miracle, just as unlikely as a valley of brittle bones becoming an army of the living God. The same Spirit "who raised Jesus from the dead" is at work within you "to fulfill his good purpose" through you (Romans 8:11; Philippians 2:13). He is the reason your future is brighter than your past.

Gracious Lord, my life is yours. I place it in your hands to do with as you please.

WHAT GOD'S WORD ACCOMPLISHES

"My word that goes out from my mouth: It will not return to me empty, but will accomplish what I desire and achieve the purpose for which I sent it."

ISAIAH 55:11

There must be something in the mind of a toddler that filters out words like "Don't climb on that!" "Spit that out! That's not food!" and "It's time to clean up!" If you have small children, then you know what it's like to have your words fall to the ground without having accomplished their purpose. If only small children knew every word a loving parent speaks to them is for their good.

In much the same way, the words our Father speaks are for our good, but unlike the warnings and commands we give to our children, his words never fall flat. They always accomplish their purpose. It's been this way from the beginning. When God said, "Let there be light" (Genesis 1:3), light appeared. Then he proceeded to speak all of creation into being. The effectiveness of his word is not limited to the six days of creation either. He spoke promises to Adam and Eve, Noah, the patriarchs, and the prophets, and not a single one was empty. Later, when God the Son appeared, he spoke to the wind and the waves, and they died down (Matthew 8:23–27). He commanded demons and diseases, and they fled (Luke 4:33–36; 7:1–10). He called the dead back to life, and they obeyed (John 11:43–44).

The Word of God that we hold in our hands—the Bible—is no less potent. The promises and warnings God gives us in Scripture are just as powerful and effective. God has not changed; he still calls new realities into being. He still commands the impossible.

When King Josiah heard the words of the book of the law, he tore his robes in grief and then reformed an entire nation (2 Kings 22:3–23:25). When the Ethiopian eunuch tripped over a description of the Savior in Isaiah 53, it sparked a conversation that changed the course of his life (Acts 8:26–39). And when the Bereans searched the Hebrew Scriptures, they believed Paul's message about Jesus of Nazareth (17:10–12).

It is not by chance or coincidence that you are reading his Word. Though the Bible may not have been written *to* you, it was written *for* you. You are meant to read it, meant to be changed by it. Let his commandments shape your life. Let his wisdom renew your mind. Let his promises awaken your heart. But most of all, let his love wash over you.

Holy God, I receive your Word. Accomplish your good purposes for my life.

THE SPIRIT OF THE GREATER THINGS

Just as Jesus was coming up out of the water,
he saw heaven being torn open
and the Spirit descending on him like a dove.

MARK 1:10

God wasn't kidding when he said the Son "made himself nothing" (Philippians 2:7). By all accounts, Jesus was a peasant—a tradesman from an obscure village in the backwater of the Roman Empire. In a crowd, he would be just another bearded Jewish face. And yet he was God in the flesh. Even so, his emptiness went deeper than his place in this world. Though he was God, Jesus did not avail himself of his divine privilege. Instead, he yielded to the Father (John 5:19). He also waited upon the Spirit.

At Jesus' baptism, the Father spoke, the Spirit alighted on the Son, and a short while later, Jesus announced, "The Spirit of the Lord is on me, because he has anointed me to proclaim good news to the poor. He has sent me to proclaim freedom for the prisoners and recovery of sight for the blind, to set the oppressed free, to proclaim the year of the Lord's favor" (Luke 4:18–19). When the Holy Spirit descended upon Jesus at his baptism (Mark 1:10), it marked the beginning of his Spirit-empowered ministry.

You see, while Jesus was, is, and will never cease to be God, the miracles and wonders he performed during his three and a half years of public ministry were not the results of his divine nature; they were, instead, done through the power of the Holy Spirit at work in his life. In other words, it was the Spirit of God set ablaze within his humanity that opened the ears of the deaf, turned water into wine, and multiplied fish and bread.

At one point in his ministry, Jesus gave authority to the Twelve, and he gave them these instructions: "Heal the sick, raise the dead, cleanse those who have leprosy, drive out demons" (Matthew 10:8). In short, "Now, go do what you've seen me do." Later, when he was preparing his friends for his impending departure, he assured them, "Whoever believes in me will do the works I have been doing, and they will do even greater things than these, because I am going to the Father" (John 14:12).

I know. It can be hard to wrap one's mind around: the same Holy Spirit that descended upon Jesus at his baptism now resides inside of you. His divine power pulses through your human form. There is no limit to what he can do in and through your life as you yield to him.

Spirit of the living God, fill me anew. Make me a vessel of the greater works Jesus promised.

TO LIVE IN FAITH

Do not merely listen to the word,
and so deceive yourselves.
Do what it says.

JAMES 1:22

If you were on trial for being a Christian, would there be enough evidence to convict you? Sadly, there are many professing believers today who would likely beat the rap and walk free. In each case, the prosecutor would not be able to find witnesses willing to testify that the defendant lived his or her daily life according to God's Word.

Too many of us have fooled ourselves into believing the gospel is like some sort of fantasy magic: a few words spoken in prayer at just the right time and—*poof*—eternal salvation. We tell ourselves, *Tuck that memory away for when doubts creep up, but don't get bogged down trying to attempt a life change here and now. God will make everything better in heaven.* But the truth is that saving faith is always active faith. We are indeed saved by faith alone, but true faith is never alone; it always blossoms into a changed life.

Jesus' half brother James wrote, "Faith by itself, if it is not accompanied by action, is dead" (2:17). He compared a person who listens to God's Word but doesn't obey it to someone who looks in the mirror and immediately forgets what he has seen (1:23–24). Such a person doesn't know to remove the gruesome bit of lettuce caught between his two front teeth. He doesn't realize he has cut himself shaving and that blood is sliding down his neck and onto his shirt. Of course, the Word of God is more than a mirror. It does much more than tell us how to clean ourselves up outwardly. Scripture reveals the hope we have in Jesus, it directs our steps so that we can live in freedom, and it shows us the way to abundant life.

As children of God, we should know our Bible. But what a tragedy it would be to learn the kings of Judah and Israel, the miracles of Jesus, and the itineraries of Paul's missionary journeys, all the while forgetting that God created us to be a part of the story! We are meant to live out the truth of God's Word in our own day and in our own corner of creation.

Jesus instructed his followers to pray that God's "will be done, on earth as it is in heaven" (Matthew 6:10). Scripture contains your marching orders so that you can be a part of answering that prayer. As you read, feel your worth as a child of the King and prepare to live boldly for Jesus in this world.

Father, kindle a fire within me. Make me an agent of heaven here on earth.

ALL GOD'S PEOPLE

Moses replied, "Are you jealous for my sake?
I wish that all the LORD's people were prophets
and that the LORD would put his Spirit on them!"

NUMBERS 11:29

Have you ever binge-watched a television show? It's then, when you see years of a show strung together in such a short span, that you notice things the casual viewer might not. It could be that a throwaway line in season one pays off big time in the final few episodes, or perhaps plot points that seemed to be going nowhere for three seasons suddenly come together in a satisfying way. Whatever the particulars, it becomes clear that you've been watching something that has been carefully thought out from the start.

The Bible has many human authors. Each one in turn picked up a stylus and wrote "as they were carried along by the Holy Spirit" (2 Peter 1:21). And when their time on earth was through, their involvement in the grand story of redemption ceased. But the Holy Spirit of God superintended the entire project, from the first words of Genesis to the final words of Revelation. We shouldn't be surprised, then, when a sentence uttered in one era predicts an event that will change the world centuries later.

God had just poured out his Spirit on seventy elders of Israel, but two of the men were not at the tent of meeting; they were in the camp with the people. So when the Spirit came upon them, they prophesied out in the open. Joshua wanted them stopped, perhaps because he thought their anointing might be seen as a threat to Moses' leadership. But Moses wasn't concerned about that: "I wish that all the LORD's people were prophets and that the LORD would put his Spirit on them!" (Numbers 11:29). Little did he know that was precisely God's plan.

When the Holy Spirit fell on men and women gathered together on Pentecost (Acts 2:1–4), it marked the beginning of a new era. From that point on, all of God's people would be vessels of the Holy Spirit, equipped and empowered to do his work in the world. Whenever a person turns to Jesus in faith, the Spirit takes up residence.

God has plans for your life—and not just for your future life but for today, for this very hour. That is why he has given you his Spirit. He will provide everything you need to have, bring to mind everything you need to know, and give you the words you don't know to speak.

Holy Spirit, lead me, guide me, and speak through me.
I yield myself to you.

TRUSTWORTHY AND TRUE

"Every word of God is flawless;
he is a shield to those who take refuge in him."
PROVERBS 30:5

It goes without saying: if God is truly God, the all-powerful and all-knowing Lord of the universe, then he doesn't make mistakes. That means he's never uttered a foolish word, spoken out of turn, committed an awkward gaffe, or gotten tongue-tied. Every time he speaks, he is intentional and on point. Everything he says is true and without a hint of error. To put it succinctly, "Every word of God is flawless."

The Hebrew word translated "flawless" refers to precious metals that have been put through the refiner's fire. The words of the Lord are "like silver purified in a crucible, like gold refined seven times" (Psalm 12:6). Every impurity and imperfection has been burned away. What's left is clean and uncontaminated, honest and pure. But, of course, the words of God have never been put into the crucible. There were never any imperfections to remove. His words came perfect and flawless from his lips.

When something is pure, we can trust and rely upon it. It's the reason pure gold is valuable everywhere. We must never forget that what we have in God's Word far surpasses gold (Psalm 19:10). Even if the whole world falls apart and every institution and authority crumbles, God's precious Word will stand. It will not let us down. It will not fail us. Because of that, God is our refuge in the storm, our shield when we're under attack. His commandments reveal goodness, and his promises light our way home. In the pages of Scripture, we discover our need for a Savior, and if we keep reading, we'll hear the Savior's life-giving voice.

Take the Bible. Take every word of it. There are no parts to shuffle off, nothing to filter out. Be wary of those who tell you to pick and choose. Ignore anyone who believes the Bible needs to be tamed, smoothed over, or abridged. Only a fool would choose to toss aside words of life.

Are you discouraged? Be encouraged by God's unfailing love for you (see Psalm 13:5). Are you ashamed? Read about how you can trade in your shame for joy (see Isaiah 61:7). In need of direction? Hear the Good Shepherd calling you into his fold (see John 10:27). Ready to move beyond the darkness? Step into the light of truth (see Psalm 119:105). In a world filled with voices vying for your attention and allegiance, don't settle for anything less than the flawless words of God.

Heavenly Father, your Word is faithful and true. Help me never to take it for granted.

A DRINK OF HOPE

May the God of hope fill you with all joy and peace as you trust in him, so that you may overflow with hope by the power of the Holy Spirit.

ROMANS 15:13

Hope is like fresh water. We need it to survive. But all too often, it's not until we find ourselves out in the desert that we realize just how precious hope really is—and how reckless we've been with it.

We need hope so badly that, as a species, we're tempted to tell ourselves whatever we need to hear just to keep going. But apart from Christ, most of this is just wishful thinking. On our own, we have no guarantee that better days are ahead, no reason to assume our situations are going to improve. Biblical hope, though, has nothing to do with the power of positive thinking. It's grounded in the character of God (Psalm 33:18), activated by the promises of God (Acts 26:6), and confirmed through the mighty acts of God (2 Corinthians 1:10).

The Holy Spirit at work within us is our catalyst for hope. He fills us with the love of God, brings us joy in the midst of hardship, and grants us "the peace of God, which transcends all understanding" (Philippians 4:7). As we taste the character of God in these blessings, we recognize deep down that he is good, no matter what the world might tell us. The Spirit also brings to our minds God's good promises as detailed in the Scriptures. We know we are not at home in this present world, so whatever we face today, we can have confidence that our future is brighter than the sun. And finally, the Holy Spirit brings power into our everyday lives. On one day, he may make us conduits for healing or the proclamation of truth. On another day, he may use our faith to break down strongholds or take back territory from the enemies of God. However the Spirit works through us, as we yield to him, we "overflow with hope" (Romans 15:13).

Though you were made to be a creature who thrives on hope, this world is in short supply of the stuff. But God, in his goodness, has given you his Holy Spirit, who is "Christ in you, the hope of glory" (Colossians 1:27). Hope is like fresh water for those who thirst. Pray that the Spirit within you will make your life a refreshing oasis for everyone you meet.

My hope is in you, God. May it rise up inside of me and spill out wherever I go.

THE SWORD FROM THE SPIRIT

Take the helmet of salvation
and the sword of the Spirit,
which is the word of God.

EPHESIANS 6:17

Y ou may recall the old schoolyard maxim "Sticks and stones may break my bones, but words can never hurt me." It may sound like basic wisdom, but anyone who's lived more than a few years on this earth knows it's rubbish. Words are powerful. They can wound. Some can even kill. It's no wonder King David described the vicious tongues of his enemies as "sharp swords" (Psalm 57:4).

When stabbed, our impulse is to stab right back. However, the New Testament tells us that "our struggle is not against flesh and blood, but against the rulers, against the authorities, against the powers of this dark world and against the spiritual forces of evil in the heavenly realms" (Ephesians 6:12). The battle between good and evil is being fought in the heavenly places and here in our world. There are enemies in the unseen realm influencing everything that happens here on earth. The people who intend to harm us with their words are not our real enemies; their souls are instead the battleground where much of the war is being waged.

So how do we fight an unseen enemy? With a sword forged in heaven—"the sword of the Spirit, which is the word of God" (v. 17). The Word of God is "of the Spirit" because it was he who breathed it out (2 Timothy 3:16). It is, therefore, a force to be reckoned with. The Greek word translated "sword" refers to a short blade Roman soldiers would use for hand-to-hand combat. It is first a defensive weapon, for with the Word of God on our lips, we are able to fend off the accusations of our enemy as we declare that our sins have been paid for at Calvary. But it is also an offensive weapon, for it is the gospel that rescues lost people from the kingdom of darkness (Colossians 1:13) and, in so doing, recovers territory from demonic forces.

Armed with the sword of the Spirit, you are a warrior for the kingdom of God. Whether or not you realize it, you have been called into battle. "Be strong and courageous. Do not be afraid or terrified…for the LORD your God goes with you; he will never leave you nor forsake you" (Deuteronomy 31:6). Never forget that the sword you brandish—the Word of God—has the power to silence the lies of the enemy and shape eternal destinies.

God of angel armies, help me to know the weight of the sword I carry—and help me to wield it well.

INSIGHTS FROM HEAVEN

The Spirit searches all things,
even the deep things of God.

1 CORINTHIANS 2:10

Every person you ever meet is a mystery. Sure, there may be things you pick up on when you first catch a glimpse—their height and hair color, maybe even an insight or two into how they conduct themselves in public—but you won't really know them until you form a relationship with them. And even then, much of what you'll learn about people will depend on what they reveal to you. Secrets from the past are usually locked up, and inner thoughts stay hidden away. Not everything unseen is dark, of course. There are memories so precious that people keep them in their mind's vault, beautiful dreams and desires so personal they remain unspoken for fear of others misunderstanding.

Attend a funeral, and you will see how a person shared certain pieces of themselves with their children, other pieces with their longtime friends, and still others with their professional colleagues. No one, not even their spouse, got to appreciate everything. Each human being is an island, "for who knows a person's thoughts except their own spirit within them?" (v. 11).

God himself is a mystery, and yet he invites us into a place of true intimacy with him. In fact, it is possible to know the Lord more deeply than we know anyone else. The Holy Spirit, who lives inside of us, is his Spirit. He knows the mind and heart of the one who carved out the oceans, invented butterflies, and painted the stars in the night sky. The Spirit seeks out and reveals to us "the deep things of God" so that we might know, in the very core of our being, what he has done for us.

To be connected to our Creator through his Spirit brings wisdom and insight beyond anything this world has to offer. At certain times, the Spirit may equip us with supernatural knowledge about things otherwise unknowable; at other times, he may provide us with a depth of understanding well beyond our years. Our job is simply to listen for his voice. "Whether you turn to the right or to the left, your ears will hear a voice behind you, saying, 'This is the way; walk in it'" (Isaiah 30:21).

You have not been left to wander through this world, to figure out life on your own. Instead, through the Spirit, "the knowledge of the secrets of the kingdom of heaven has been given to you" (Matthew 13:11). Live as though you have a constant connection to heaven—because you do.

Father, my understanding is limited and frail. Renew my mind as only you can.

THE JESUS BOOK

"You study the Scriptures diligently because
you think that in them you have eternal life.
These are the very Scriptures that testify about me,
yet you refuse to come to me to have life."

JOHN 5:39–40

In the 2000 movie *Cast Away,* Tom Hanks plays Chuck Noland, a FedEx systems engineer who finds himself stranded on an island in the middle of the ocean after a plane crash. Very quickly, his life becomes all about survival.

As FedEx packages from the plane wash up on shore, Noland begins collecting them, and he eventually opens them all except one. The special package is emblazoned with golden wings, and it becomes a symbol of hope for Noland. That unopened, undelivered package gives him a sense of purpose: he has to get off the island in order to deliver it.

When Noland finally does make it back to civilization, he has the package in tow. He eventually delivers it, but since the recipient is not home, we don't get to see what's inside. As the story goes, the box's contents don't really matter; the package itself was enough to keep Noland going. But of course, the film's audience has long wondered what was inside.

Several years ago, FedEx had a little fun with one of its commercials, depicting a scene in which Noland (not played by Hanks this time) delivers the package and asks the smiling recipient what's inside. She replies, "Nothing, really. Just a satellite phone, GPS locator, fishing rod, water purifier, and some seeds."

Many people treat the Bible like that lost FedEx package. It's a symbol of hope. They cherish it. They read it. They study it. But they never discover the salvation inside. The Scriptures are not an end in themselves; they were given to us so that we might know Jesus Christ and, in him, find life. From the first "In the beginning" of Genesis 1:1 to the final "Amen" of Revelation 22:21, it's all there to help us find the Son—and the way home. Jesus himself is the key: "And beginning with Moses and all the Prophets, he explained to them what was said in all the Scriptures concerning himself" (Luke 24:27).

God did not give you his Word so that you might have yet another homework assignment added to your already busy day. Instead, he breathed the Scriptures into this world and sovereignly placed them into your hands so that you might fall ever deeper in love with Jesus.

Precious Jesus, as I open up my Bible, I also open up my heart to you. Meet with me in this place.

HOLY HEARTACHE

Do not grieve the Holy Spirit of God,
with whom you were sealed for the day of
redemption.

EPHESIANS 4:30

It's getting more and more difficult to remember
that there was once a time when virtually all people
endeavored to live at peace. A person's reputation and
standing in the community could be measured by the
amount of respect and kindness he or she doled out.
These days, however, social media has made it "safe" to
say whatever we want to people we've never even met.
Hiding behind a screen, it's easy to feel untouchable,
and it's easy to pretend the people we've offended are
just names and avatars and flat representations of a
political persuasion with which we disagree.

Of course, if we were to pause for a few seconds'
worth of deep reflection, we'd recognize such thinking
is nonsense. Dismissive words and hateful speech are
no less damaging when transmitted via broadband
wires and cell phone signals than when shouted in
someone's face. People really do matter, even people
we've never met in real life. How much more, then,
should we account for the feelings of the Spirit of God?

That notion might seem strange at first. After all, the Holy Spirit is sovereign, all-knowing, and powerful beyond measure. Is it really possible that our words and actions can cause him grief?

The Holy Spirit is not some detached, impersonal force. He is a living person who thinks and feels more deeply than we do. When we step off the path he's leading us down, we bring him sorrow. He knows what's best for us. He wants what's best for us. Our sin brings him pain. The ancient Israelites did this in the wilderness—"they rebelled and grieved [God's] Holy Spirit" (Isaiah 63:10)—and they quickly found themselves in the dangerous place of opposing the Lord.

Your sin is not a private matter. It affects all of your relationships, including your relationship with the Holy Spirit inside of you. God's love for you, of course, is not weakened by your sins. The Spirit himself is the seal of your salvation. But the peace and joy of that salvation will dry up, and the Comforter will cease to bring you comfort. That's no way for a Christian to live. So, walk closely with the Spirit and repent at the slightest hint of sin creeping up in your heart.

Just as the Spirit led those early Israelites through the wilderness to the promised land, he's now leading you. Try not to trip on the way; it breaks his heart.

Holy Spirit, forgive me for all the times I've caused you grief. Thank you for not giving up on me.

OUR DAILY BREAD

Jesus answered, "It is written: 'Man shall not live on bread alone, but on every word that comes from the mouth of God.'"

MATTHEW 4:4

Most of us think nothing of reaching out for the blessing of food three times a day (and a few other times besides). But if, say, tomorrow our refrigerators and pantries were mysteriously bare and our favorite restaurants and diners were closed with no explanation, we might begin to panic. We'd say we were "starving" even though a single day without a bite would not bring us to that low estate. I'd imagine that by midafternoon, more than a few of us would be crying out to God in prayer, pleading with him to provide our daily bread. And yet, how many of us have experienced a day without reading or meditating on Scripture with no such distress?

Jesus said the Word of God is just as essential to life as eating. He made this statement, drawing from Deuteronomy 8:3, after going forty days without a morsel. To put it mildly, "he was hungry" (Matthew 4:2). Even so, when the devil tempted him to transform stones into loaves of bread, he pushed back.

It wasn't that Jesus believed eating was somehow unholy, nor was he against using supernatural power to sidestep baking. In his coming ministry, he would feed thousands by multiplying bread and fish. Rather, it was that Jesus was completely yielded to the Father, so he refused to satisfy his hunger on his own terms; he would wait upon God instead.

The ancient Israelites in the wilderness had grumbled and complained against the Lord when they were hungry. In response, God began providing manna from heaven each day to teach them that daily bread comes from him. He did this so they would know it was him they needed, not mere food. Jesus walked in this truth every day of his earthly life, and now he calls us to do the same.

We need food to sustain us and keep us healthy, but eating should also serve as a thrice-daily reminder that God is our provider. What we need more than bread or meat or chocolate is the Lord himself. We must learn to lean on him every day, all day. And we start by savoring his Word.

God did not make you to live on bread alone. Partake of spiritual food. Eat from the Word of God regularly, and you'll soon be craving it in between meals, proclaiming with the psalmist, "How sweet are your words to my taste, sweeter than honey to my mouth!" (Psalm 119:103).

Sustainer of life, satisfy me with your good Word, for I am hungry.

HOLY SPIRIT HOST

Do you not know that your bodies are
temples of the Holy Spirit, who is in you,
whom you have received from God?

1 CORINTHIANS 6:19

It began with the sound of teeth crunching into forbidden fruit. A short time later, we human beings found ourselves driven away from God's presence, even as the Lord found ways of drawing near to us. He spoke to the patriarchs, at times appearing to them in human or angelic form. He showed up in signs and wonders to rescue and redeem. He delivered his messages through burning bushes and donkeys and prophets—all so we would know he cares for us. And, of course, "in these last days he has spoken to us by his Son" (Hebrews 1:2).

It's a pattern we see throughout Scripture: the justice of God keeps sinners from returning home, but the love of God keeps him reaching out to make his home with us. We see this most clearly in the tabernacle and, later, in the temple. God dwelled in the midst of his people, but the people couldn't get too close, at least not without the shedding of blood. Even then, it was only the high priest who could enter the Most Holy Place, where the manifest presence of God dwelled—and that was only on one special day each year (Leviticus 16).

So, imagine the delight of the first Christians when they became living, breathing temples of God. No longer was God's residence on earth confined to a room at the center of the temple in the city of Jerusalem. Beginning at Pentecost, the Holy Spirit took up residence within the people of God, each one becoming an outpost of heaven in this fallen world.

No distance exists between the Lord and those of us who love him. There is no longer the need for an earthly priest to make intercession before we can come close; Jesus Christ is the high priest who "always lives to intercede" (Hebrews 7:25). And animal sacrifices are no longer necessary either, for "we have been made holy through the sacrifice of the body of Jesus Christ once for all" (10:10).

Your body is a sacred space, a walking, talking temple of the Lord God Almighty. Therefore, pour out everything you are as an offering of praise. Become "a living sacrifice, holy and pleasing to God" (Romans 12:1). Host the Holy Spirit with your life, each and every day.

Holy One of Israel, I love your presence. My heart beats to worship you.

THE WORD MADE FLESH

In the beginning was the Word,
and the Word was with God,
and the Word was God.

JOHN 1:1

Words are spoken, sent forth to accomplish their purpose. And yet words are inseparable from the person who speaks them. Words are a bit of ourselves let out into the world to connect and to influence. They are a part of us, an extension of our being, and they are so, so powerful.

In the very beginning, God spoke. His Word went forth, and the lights came on. Waters parted. Lush greens and yellows and reds and browns sprouted up from newly freed earth. The sun, moon, and stars took their places in cold space. Birds flapped and winged their way through the atmosphere. Fish flopped and flitted their way through the depths. Beasts of every size and shape scratched and galloped and strutted across their new home. And humanity drew a breath.

The Son was the Word the Father spoke at the dawn of time. "For in him all things were created: things in heaven and on earth, visible and invisible" (Colossians 1:16). The Word is God himself but also, somehow, distinct from God. He is uncreated; he was there with God at the beginning. "Through him all things were made" (John 1:3). And he is the source of life, the very light of humanity (v. 4).

But let's not forget that a word from the Lord is also a message. God spoke through his prophets to warn the people of sin's consequences and to make his kindness known. Jesus is the ultimate message: the way of salvation writ large (14:6), the accurate picture of the Father we all need to see (12:45; Hebrews 1:3), and the path that leads to life and wholeness (John 10:9).

So, then, what should we make of the Word of God written down, the Holy Scriptures handed down to us through the ages? The Bible is, of course, not divine, but the Son of God is forever intertwined with the Scriptures. Jesus said he was the fulfillment of the Law and the Prophets (Matthew 5:17). He also walked a pair of traveling disciples through the Hebrew Bible and showed them all the places where he could be found (Luke 24:25–27).

You have been given the Word (the Bible) so that you might encounter the Word (Jesus Christ). The breadcrumbs of redemption spilled lavishly from Genesis to Revelation are there to lead you to the Son. Seek his heart. Listen for his voice. Hold fast to him, child of the King.

Jesus, Word from the Father, bring a new creation into this world. Start with me.

THE HARVEST WILL BE AMAZING

Not only so, but we ourselves, who have the firstfruits of the Spirit, groan inwardly as we wait eagerly for our adoption to sonship, the redemption of our bodies.

ROMANS 8:23

There's something about the first taste of a backyard garden in the spring. For weeks, it's been nothing but dirt and seeds and leafy sprouts. There was the business of preparing the soil and planting and watering. Then, all at once—or at least it seems that way—there are sumptuous greens and reds and yellows and blues. That first raspberry tastes sweeter than expected. The cucumbers seem bigger than last year's crop. And the tomatoes are a deeper shade of red than you had anticipated.

When the first bits of the season's harvest are good, there's reason to believe the whole garden will be spectacular. This is true in the backyard, but it's also true in the grand story of redemption God is writing with our lives. You see, you and I have been promised an eternal harvest, a crop beyond our wildest imaginations (1 Corinthians 2:9), and God is so good that he has given us the firstfruits today.

Someday, our full adoption as sons and daughters of the King will be realized. On that day, we will take our places in our forever home with the Lord of all creation. In that glory, we will no longer struggle under the weight of these perishable frames, slowed by age and hollowed out by disease (15:42–44). We will be raised to new life in transformed bodies that "shine like the brightness of the heavens" (Daniel 12:2–3). Heaven and nature will sing as all things are made new, and we will join in the chorus.

Until then, the firstfruits of the Spirit, which we received when we first trusted Christ, remind us that the harvest to come is "immeasurably more than all we ask or imagine" (Ephesians 3:20). The Holy Spirit—the gift of God within us—is a taste of the kingdom. It's as though eternity itself has reached back in time to help us keep our eyes fixed on the promises of God.

You were made for more. There are joys unending waiting for you on the other side of this life. The Father has given you his Holy Spirit as a taste of the glory Jesus purchased for you at the cross. Your privilege, no matter your circumstances, is to live in unrelenting hope. That is God's will for you.

Prince of Peace, you are so good to me. Help me to live a life of gratitude for the harvest to come.

THE REST OF THE SKY'S MESSAGE

The heavens declare the glory of God;
the skies proclaim the work of his hands.

PSALM 19:1

It seems God is determined to grab our attention. Day and night, the sky serves as the biggest billboard in creation, perpetually declaring the beauty and goodness of the Lord who created it. It bids us to look up, not just to the vault above our heads but also to the God who sits on an unseen throne in the heavens beyond the heavens.

During our waking hours, brilliant blues are decorated with ten thousand combinations of billowy whites and grays. The sun gives us the time of day as it paces across the final frontier, all the while delivering the light we need to survive and love and create and wonder. When the sky is overcome with clouds entirely, the light is filtered through another glory—a fierce blanket of provision and power.

In the cool of night, we find that the same sky under which we scurried just a few hours earlier is now punched through with diamonds from heaven. The moon's face, forever advancing, then retreating, guides our steps through a cobalt landscape, reminding us that the Maker of the universe has not forgotten us in the darkness.

The sky is speaking to us if only we will pause, look up, and receive its message. "For since the creation of the world God's invisible qualities—his eternal power and divine nature—have been clearly seen" (Romans 1:20).

But the sky can only say so much.

The sky will never tell us about the disease of sin coursing through our veins or the curse of death hanging over us. It will never announce the price that Jesus paid at Calvary so sinful men and women could be cleansed and forgiven. It will never speak of God's gift of the Spirit or reveal what it means to bear the image of God in all faithfulness. For these things, we need another book.

The Word of God is the rest of the message. While the majesty of the sky might quicken our hearts to seek out its Maker, creation alone will never answer the most important questions of eternity. That is why God, in his infinite kindness, has given us the Scriptures.

Cherish the Bible. Without it, you would be lost, and God would still be a stranger. The way home would still be a mystery. Never forget that Scripture was and is your invitation to know the one who painted the sky.

Father of lights, your goodness surrounds me. I long for more of you.

WHOM SHALL I FEAR?

The Spirit God gave us does not make us timid,
but gives us power, love and self-discipline.

2 TIMOTHY 1:7

There's more to be afraid of than the things that go bump in the night. For many of us, fear does not recede with the morning light. Day in and day out, we live in the shadow of the fear of failure, the fear of rejection, or the fear of being alone. In this way, fear becomes a way of life. These fears envelop us and compel us to behave a certain way to avoid getting hurt. Worse than that, they rob us of the freedom and joy we were meant to walk in.

Fear comes from living in the valley of the shadow of death. Our world has no shortage of pain and suffering, isolation and defeat. We're surrounded on every side. Though we were placed in the green pastures of Eden's garden at the beginning, sin thrust our species out into the wild lands of uncertainty and lack. Our only hope is to find rest in the presence of God.

God knows this. It's why, once Christ's shed blood had cleansed us from the stains of sin, he sent his Spirit to live within us, to comfort and refresh us, to silence our fears. This taste of Eden we know as the Holy Spirit provides for us and prepares us so that we can be truly free (2 Corinthians 3:17). This freedom is not the sort that indulges our sinful nature. Rather, it's the freedom to love and be loved, to walk in the truth, to know our value as children of the King, and to see other people as sacred image-bearers. The Spirit draws us to God (Galatians 4:6), shapes our thoughts and desires so they align with heaven (Ezekiel 36:27), and equips each of us to carry out the unique mission God has for us in this broken world (Colossians 1:9–10).

Are you afraid? "The one who is in you is greater than the one who is in the world" (1 John 4:4). The Spirit of comfort and power came to set you free from the fear of death and all the fears of this life. He wants to cleanse your heart of any fear that threatens to rob you of the abundant life God has for you.

Spirit of peace, I cast aside all my fears in the knowledge that you are always with me.

An Invitation to Go Deeper

Now the Berean Jews were of more noble character than those in Thessalonica, for they received the message with great eagerness and examined the Scriptures every day to see if what Paul said was true.

Acts 17:11

Perhaps you've been warned not to look too carefully at your Bible, told that if you were really to study it with a critical eye, you'd find discrepancies and contradictions throughout. Maybe you've even read that Scripture doesn't mix well with science or politics, that the best thing to do is to keep your faith a private matter.

While it's certainly true that the Bible wasn't written to answer every possible question we might have, the Word of God does not need protection from sincere inquiry. We need not fear digging into those passages that, on the surface, may appear difficult or troubling. True faith, despite what you may have heard, presses deep into the pages of Scripture, examining and reexamining everything in its light. Only a book produced by the Spirit of God would prove faithful time and time again (see Numbers 23:19)—and that is exactly what billions of people across the continents and down through the ages have discovered.

The Bereans of Acts 17 stand at the beginning of a long line of careful thinkers. They received the gospel with enthusiastic joy but then compared what Paul told them about Jesus' death and resurrection with what God had previously revealed in the Old Testament. Their faithful journey of discovery into Scripture did not disappoint. They came away convinced Paul's good news really was good.

Contrary to what some have suggested, it is not our place to decide which parts of Scripture we will accept as truth and which we will cast aside. Rather, we are called to do the opposite: to yield in submission to everything the Word of God tells us and to judge our own actions and choices by the plain teaching of the Lord. Honest inquiry does not bring our doubts to hold court over Scripture; rather, it seeks a more complete picture of God's heart.

You do not need to protect your Bible from difficult questions. Like the Bereans, test that what you are hearing resonates with what God has already said. Dig in, read, and study, all the while knowing that God's Word is perfect (Psalm 18:30). When you receive it in faith and humility, Scripture will not lead you astray but will bring you closer to your heavenly Father, who loves you.

Holy Spirit, guide my heart and my mind as I read your Word. Reveal the truth to me.

CARRIED BEFORE THE THRONE

In the same way, the Spirit helps us in our weakness. We do not know what we ought to pray for, but the Spirit himself intercedes for us through wordless groans.

ROMANS 8:26

Sometimes in life an honest saint is too weak to pray. In other moments, she's too heartbroken to find the words.

We should never imagine that we will travel the Christian life solely on the road to victory. We may spend seasons along the winding paths of despair and loss, long sojourns under the shadow of death. God does not leave us alone on those trails, of course, but these dark stretches can leave us crushed in spirit, unable to breathe under the weight of this world. Thankfully, "the LORD is close to the brokenhearted" (Psalm 34:18). For in these times of loneliness, the Spirit gives us one of his greatest gifts.

The Spirit of God is the friend who knows us better than we know ourselves, and he lifts our concerns up to the highest heaven, interceding on our behalf in ways so powerful that no words can do his prayer justice. He does not despise our weakness or demand we pull ourselves together but instead binds up our wounds and brings us to our healer. When we don't know what we ought to pray, he steps in to pray for us. His prayer is not lacking in any way. He prays for precisely what we need—custom-made blessings at just the right moment to strengthen us and draw us closer to the heart of the Father.

Someday, when we step into glory and see long-hidden mysteries revealed, I imagine we'll marvel at all the times the Spirit of God intervened in our lives. On countless days when we were too feeble to stand on our own two feet spiritually, it was the Holy Spirit who picked us up and carried us before the throne of grace. We'll scarcely remember having been so weak because of the mercies secured on our behalf.

When the darkness comes and will not lift, know you are not alone. When you don't know how or what to pray, know the Spirit is praying for you. And when new strength comes, thank the Spirit who interceded on your behalf.

Comforter, thank you for carrying me when I cannot carry myself. I am eternally grateful.

FINDING YOURSELF IN THE PAGES OF SCRIPTURE

"I will raise up Cyrus in my righteousness:
I will make all his ways straight.
He will rebuild my city and set my exiles free,
but not for a price or reward, says the LORD Almighty."

ISAIAH 45:13

Have you ever seen yourself in the pages of Scripture while reading God's Word? When we come to Jesus, we become a part of God's chosen nation, whether or not we have a drop of Jewish blood in our veins (Ephesians 2:13). That means that the Old and New Testaments are our family history, our origin story. We look back on a long line of men and women who stood in faith and endured till they were called home—and now it's our turn to stand.

A king once found himself as he read the scrolls of Hebrew Scripture, specifically the book of Isaiah. The passage in question was written perhaps a hundred years before this king was born. And yet this passage contained his actual name: "I am the LORD, who made all things,…who says of Cyrus, 'He is my shepherd, and he shall fulfill all my purpose'; saying of Jerusalem, 'She shall be built,' and of the temple, 'Your foundation shall be laid'" (Isaiah 44:24, 28 ESV).

Long before Cyrus was a figure on the world stage, long before the people of Judah were taken into exile, and long before the city of Jerusalem was destroyed by Nebuchadnezzar, God's Word predicted King Cyrus of Persia would issue an order for Jerusalem to be rebuilt. The Lord even got the smallest details right, noting that the temple itself would not be completed in Cyrus' day but only the foundation (see Ezra 5:16).

The Jewish historian Josephus records that when Cyrus saw his own name written in the Hebrew Scriptures and the monumental task God had entrusted to him in those pages, he was so taken aback that he made it his mission to fulfill the prophecy. But of course, God knew this was exactly how Cyrus would react and how this prophecy would come to pass in the first place.

Though you may not find your name written in the Bible, you are there. The Spirit of God was thinking of you when he inspired these words: "But you are a chosen people, a royal priesthood, a holy nation, God's special possession, that you may declare the praises of him who called you out of darkness into his wonderful light" (1 Peter 2:9). Now, live out your calling.

Sovereign Lord, who knew me before time began, thank you for writing me into your story.

WHERE THE WIND BLOWS

"The wind blows wherever it pleases.
You hear its sound, but you cannot tell
where it comes from or where it is going.
So it is with everyone born of the Spirit."

JOHN 3:8

On a hot summer day, an active breeze can be the difference between yard work and hard labor, between a walk in the fresh air and an endurance test. And on those days when the gusts are few and far between, the sound of the wind wafting through the leaves of distant trees can seem like a cruel taunt. Standing out under the sweltering sun, we can do nothing to draw the breeze our way; we can only be patient and hope it finds us.

In both Hebrew and Greek, the word for "wind" is the same as the word for "Spirit." And so when Jesus told Nicodemus that the Spirit of God was like the wind, it was a bit of a play on words. But wordplay aside, the untamable quality of the wind perfectly describes God's Holy Spirit. No one can summon the Spirit or predict which path he'll choose. A person who has been born of the Spirit may or may not be able to point to the specific moment when the Spirit made his home within. (The only common element in every story is faith in Christ and his saving work.) And just as there is no mistaking the sound of the wind, the Spirit's work in a person's life is also self-evident and undeniable.

Only the Spirit can transform us into the true image-bearers of God we were created to be, but the process itself is a mystery. He works in different ways in the lives of different people, slowly making us more like Jesus, "the radiance of God's glory and the exact representation of his being" (Hebrews 1:3). We need only to trust and obey and then rejoice when we feel him working on us.

In the beginning, "the Spirit of God was hovering over the waters" (Genesis 1:2), not unlike the wind, preparing the formless world beneath for the creation to come. Today, he is preparing you for the new creation, when God will renew all things (Matthew 19:28). Though you may be sweltering under the heat of this cruel world, know that the Spirit is at work to bring lasting refreshment to all who call on the name of the Lord.

Good Father, I want to be carried along by your Spirit within me. Make me sensitive to his every move.

THOROUGHLY BIBLE PEOPLE

Impress them on your children. Talk about them
when you sit at home and when you walk along the
road, when you lie down and when you get up.

DEUTERONOMY 6:7

How do you pass along the basics of your faith to
your children? According to the Bible, you do it a little
bit every day. No formal educational setting is required.
No videos or workbooks or homework needed. Not a
single talking vegetable or anthropomorphic songbook.
Instead, all you need are the everyday moments—the
carpool line, the dinner table, those precious few
minutes before bedtime, "when you sit at home and
when you walk along the road." The trick is to keep the
conversation going and to seize little moments each
day as opportunities to talk about eternal things.

But not everyone reading these words is a parent,
and this is not a book of parenting hacks. I bring up
the instructions God gave to parents in Deuteronomy
6 because they build upon something even more
foundational, something that every single follower of
the Lord needs to understand: we can only be people
who pass on the Word of God to our children—or
our coworkers, our friends, and our family—if we are
first people steeped and soaked so thoroughly in the

truth of Scripture that it proceeds from our mouths as naturally as the air we breathe.

This is a tall order, of course, and requires us to think about the Bible as more than a book we read for encouragement and inspiration. Scripture needs to become the backdrop to our lives, our favorite epic that informs our understanding of the world and ourselves. We cannot afford to think that studying the deep things of God belongs only to the pastors and theologians among us. Rather, every last one of us must become a lifelong student of God's Word. Just as God intended for each new generation, the Scriptures must become part of our everyday lives. And so, we must learn and grow a little bit more each day.

Maybe you've been studying the Bible for decades and feel at home in its pages. Or maybe you're still learning the difference between Chronicles and Corinthians. Either way, your calling is the same: to grow more in love with the author of Scripture as you spend time in the Bible's pages.

May your love for God and his Word touch everyone you meet.

Author and perfecter of my faith, teach me your Word so that I might teach others.

EMPOWERED FROM ON HIGH

"Afterward, I will pour out my Spirit on all people.
Your sons and daughters will prophesy, your old men
will dream dreams, your young men will see visions."

JOEL 2:28

In the Old Testament, the Spirit of God came upon a relatively small number of people—eccentric prophets, powerful kings, unique judges, and select craftsmen among the lot. The Spirit equipped these men and women for a certain role or task. God's hand was upon them, and God's works flowed through them for a season.

But then something amazing happened.

God made an unbelievable promise to his people. Even as he warned them of impending judgment for their reckless sin and relentless idolatry, he let them know there was a day coming when his Spirit would come to rest on all flesh, not just a chosen few. All of his people—young, old, male, female—would become vessels for his divine power and wisdom. They would be connected to God in ways they simply hadn't been before.

At Pentecost, a few days after Jesus ascended to the Father, this promise came true (Acts 2:16–21)—and it holds true today. Anyone who comes to Jesus in faith receives the Holy Spirit. God is no longer a distant stranger but a holy companion for every day of this life.

Of course, it's not that the Spirit has become common. In fact, the Spirit's presence remains reserved for kings and prophets and servants of God. The truth is that you and I and every follower of Jesus have been elevated; we are now a "royal priesthood" (1 Peter 2:9) and "ambassadors" for heaven (2 Corinthians 5:20). We are doing the work of people like Gideon and Elijah, Jeremiah and Deborah, though in our own unique contexts. Like the prophets of old, we have been called to speak God's message (Matthew 28:18–20). We have been given spiritual manifestations in order to bless the community of faith (1 Corinthians 12:7) and, by extension, the world at large.

God has poured out his Spirit upon you. You have received an immeasurable gift, one that many of God's people down through the ages could scarcely have imagined. God himself is at work within you—to speak to you and through you. Always remember: the calling is as amazing as the gift. God has given you a unique assignment and has empowered you to do his will here on earth.

Ancient of Days, speak to me through your Spirit. Move me, use me, and accomplish your purposes through me.

THE WAY OF THE WORD

The word of God is alive and active. Sharper than any
double-edged sword, it penetrates even to dividing
soul and spirit, joints and marrow; it judges the
thoughts and attitudes of the heart.

HEBREWS 4:12

There's something about being out on the open
road, seeing new bits of creation for the first time, not
knowing what's around the next bend. For those of us
with wanderlust, it's exhilarating; for the homebodies
among us, it's daunting. But one thing is certain: each
one of us is on a journey, whether or not we realize it.

From cover to cover, the Bible speaks of
two paths before us and a fork in the road at every
juncture. It doesn't matter where we start out; we all
have the same choice: we can either take the path of
righteousness, which is the narrow way of obedience
to our Creator, or we can follow the well-traveled way
of fools, the broad highway to destruction (Psalm 1:6;
Matthew 7:13–14).

Reading through the Old Testament, we watch
God's people choose the wrong path over and over
again. But rather than shake our heads and imagine
we'd get it right if we were in their place, we ought to
remember that "everything that was written in the past

was written to teach us" (Romans 15:4). We are meant to learn from the mistakes of the Israelites. God has given us their stories so that we might choose the right path when it's our turn.

An entire generation of Israelites missed out on the rest and refreshment of the promised land because they did not believe the word of the Lord. Rather than trust him to meet their needs, they grumbled and complained against him. And so, that entire generation, save Joshua and Caleb, perished in the desert without ever receiving the new home God promised.

Now it's our turn. "Let us, therefore, make every effort to enter that rest" (Hebrews 4:11). Like the Israelites before us, we will be judged by what God has spoken. The words of the Lord are not past and gone but are instead "alive and active" (v. 12), and they penetrate the deepest part of our being. Those who ignore the Word of God are judged by it.

Every day, you have a choice to make: you can either live according to God's Word, or you can go your own way. There is life and peace and rest in one direction, anxiety and fear and death in the other. The choice is always before you, so choose wisely.

King of Glory, increase my faith so that I trust you more each day. I live to hear your voice.

THE GIFT THAT'S JUST FOR YOU

There are different kinds of gifts,
but the same Spirit distributes them.

1 CORINTHIANS 12:4

All it takes is one Christmas with small children to discover individual gifts matter. Sure, certain presents, few and far between, work equally well for a two-year-old and a nine-year-old. Who doesn't like that giant tin of assorted popcorn that's only available during the holidays? But a few months after the stockings and lights come down, it will be the tailored and personal gifts they still reach for—the presents that seem to speak to who they are as individuals. The artsy six-year-old will still be decorating the world with her art supplies, the football fan will still be sleeping with his beloved Wilson, and the young readers will still be poring over their stack of new favorite books.

When it comes to spiritual gifts, our Father knows just how to bless us—and just how to bless the church. That's why he gives us gifts according to his wisdom and knowledge. While one person might receive the gift of teaching, another has the gift of healing. Someone may get the gift of supernatural faith while another receives the gift of prophecy. And of course, some people receive a combination of gifts;

others receive one gift for a season and then grow to wield another gift at a different time. The Lord is infinitely creative when it comes to how he blesses his children.

Spiritual gifts are never impersonal. The God who formed you in the womb has always known what gifts would complement your talents, skills, and experiences, and it brings him joy to see his kids discover their place and fulfill their purpose in the fellowship of believers.

These gifts, when taken together and used according to their design, are for everyone's good. That is why Paul, in 1 Corinthians, describes Christians with their spiritual gifts as unique parts of one body (12:12–27). The eye helps the foot know where to walk; the heart supplies blood to the fingers and toes. All parts are essential; not one is wasted.

Have you unwrapped your gifts? Do you know how the Spirit has empowered you? If you've never discovered your spiritual gifts as a child of God, don't waste any more time. Seek the Lord and ask him to reveal how he's blessed you. Your brothers and sisters need you to use your gifts. The days are getting darker, and time is of the essence.

God of every good thing, thank you for the spiritual gifts you've given me. Help me to walk in each one.

PERFECT LIKE THE FATHER

"I tell you that unless your righteousness surpasses
that of the Pharisees and the teachers of the law, you
will certainly not enter the kingdom of heaven."

MATTHEW 5:20

For years, I had a recurring dream about being back
in school. It's late in the semester, and I discover there's
a class I signed up for but have never attended. I've
earned a zero for every assignment I've missed, and
the final exam is today. There's no way I can cram an
entire course's worth of work into a few hours, and so
I begin to stress. There goes my grade point average.
There goes my hope of graduating. I'm done for—and
all because I spaced on my class schedule a few months
earlier. Maybe you can relate to the feeling of missing
the mark because you didn't even know where the
mark was.

When Jesus began teaching publicly, he surprised
a lot of folks by moving the mark. He said things
like, "You have heard that it was said, 'You shall not
commit adultery.' But I tell you that anyone who looks
at a woman lustfully has already committed adultery
with her in his heart" (vv. 27–28). Some people had
convinced themselves they were righteous in God's
eyes because they had obeyed the commandments and

then offered the proper sacrifices when they messed up. They hadn't murdered or committed adultery or stolen anything. But then Jesus informed them that wasn't enough.

You see, behind every one of the Ten Commandments—behind every law and precept of the Lord—is the heart of heaven. Every commandment reflects the goodness of God. In other words, if you want to know what God is like, pay attention to how he tells his children to live. What God truly wants for us is to walk the way he walks. As Jesus himself put it, "Be perfect, therefore, as your heavenly Father is perfect" (v. 48). Jesus wasn't really moving the target after all; he was showing the world why there was a target in the first place.

Thankfully, Jesus hit the bullseye for us. He followed every commandment and requirement of the law perfectly so that we can have his righteousness (2 Corinthians 5:21). That's how, when we stand before God, our own godliness can surpass the piety of the most rigorous of Pharisees.

Chase after the heart of God in everything you do. Strive to be just like your Father. That's the life he created you for.

Jesus, beloved of the Father, thank you for showing me the way home. Help me to live as a child of heaven.

THE SPIRIT'S AGENDA

The Spirit of the LORD came powerfully upon him so that he tore the lion apart with his bare hands as he might have torn a young goat. But he told neither his father nor his mother what he had done.

JUDGES 14:6

To put things mildly, Samson had a few personality flaws. Fueled by a generous amount of lust and rage, Samson spent much of his adult life doing what seemed good to him in the moment. And yet he was a judge over Israel, "dedicated to God from the womb" for the people's deliverance (13:5).

When the Holy Spirit came upon Samson, it was with the gift of supernatural strength. He was able to take on any threat, ripping apart lions with his bare hands and slaughtering men by the thousand. If Samson lived today, we'd no doubt consider him something of a superhero, though we'd have to hold the "hero" part lightly. Samson didn't fight crime or protect the innocent; he mostly stomped on people who got in the way of his own good time. Even so, when it came time to chronicle the hall of faith, the author of Hebrews gave a nod to our biblical Hercules, Samson.

The Spirit's agenda is heaven's agenda. He did not empower Samson so that he could make time with Philistine women; rather, he granted Samson unparalleled strength so that he might destroy the fighting men from among Israel's enemies. In other words, the Spirit unleashed God's judgment upon the Philistines, and Samson was that judgment's name. Rather than waiting for Samson to become pious, the Spirit simply used his sinful tendencies to help the Lord's people. In the end, when Samson was humbled, captured, and blinded, he finally understood God's purpose for his life. His last act was to sacrifice himself in order to set the people of Israel free (16:30). For that, he's remembered as a man of faith in the New Testament.

Do not be surprised when you encounter gifted people who are still a mess, "for God's gifts and his call are irrevocable" (Romans 11:29). God doesn't usually wait for his children to clean up their acts before empowering them to serve. Each one of us is a work in progress, and yet nothing we do (or fail to do) can thwart the purposes of God. In the meantime, ask the Lord to give you a heart that seeks God's will to be done "on earth as it is in heaven" (Matthew 6:10).

Warrior of heaven, reveal the sinfulness of my heart so that my own agenda aligns with yours.

JUDGED BY SCRIPTURE

Scripture has locked up everything under the control of sin, so that what was promised, being given through faith in Jesus Christ, might be given to those who believe.

GALATIANS 3:22

The Bible details God's wonderful plan of redemption in Jesus. In that, it gives life to all who pick up, read, and believe. But the Bible does not work well as a checklist. There is no to-do list within all of Scripture that has the power to rouse us from the dead or break the curse of sin.

The commandments of God, while rich and good, can do nothing to secure our home with the Lord in eternity. In fact, these rules have just the opposite power. The law, on its own, condemns us, for not even one of us can obey it perfectly. When we attempt to follow the law of God, we only reveal our inability to do so. We show ourselves to be imperfect image-bearers of God. Not one of us represents the Lord as well as we should; we all "fall short of the glory of God" (Romans 3:23).

It seems a strange thing, doesn't it? God, in his infinite sovereignty, gave his people commandments upon commandments to follow, but the greatest purpose of those commandments was to show just how powerful sin is. The law was given to reveal their—and our—need for a Savior. To be sure, the commands of Scripture also reveal the holiness and goodness of God, but even in doing that, they demonstrate just how far away we are from his perfect standard.

That's the thing about our sinful nature: we are so broken that we don't know how broken we are. We actually imagine we can work our way back to Eden through discipline and obedience. So God, in his mercy, shows us just how far off we are. Then, he offers us grace and mercy and a Savior who was perfectly obedient. This same Savior paid sin's wages so we wouldn't have to. That's why the good news is so good. You and I have been given everything—literally everything—and the Son of God paid our tab.

Live in freedom. Walk in peace. You cannot do anything to make the Father love you any more than he already does. Your life is now joy and gratitude because Jesus has made a way home for you. Cease from your striving. Breathe deep. Christ's perfect righteousness is yours.

Lamb of God, you exchanged my sinfulness for your righteousness. You took the cross that was rightfully mine. I love you forever.

TRUTH UNFILTERED

"When he, the Spirit of truth, comes, he will guide you into all the truth. He will not speak on his own; he will speak only what he hears, and he will tell you what is yet to come."

JOHN 16:13

What is truth?" (18:38). That was Pilate's question when heaven granted him an audience with the Son of God. Today, it's a question many people are still asking. We are a species awash in information, but actual truth seems to be in short supply. Even so, as Christians, we have direct access to the truth. It fills every page of the Bible, and Jesus himself is truth (14:6). Beyond that, we have the Lord's promise that the Spirit will be our guide "into all the truth" (16:13). In that, we live at the crossroads of truth and faith. We, of all people, have reason to be confident in the worldview given to us by our Father.

Truth is a life raft floating on a sea of chaos. Sadly, many people today—even believers—would rather study the waves than hold on to that raft. In reality, there is no shortage of truth. We simply need to avail ourselves of the Spirit's guidance and the teachings of Scripture.

The Bible says, "A matter must be established by the testimony of two or three witnesses" (Deuteronomy 19:15). We have three witnesses: the Father, the Son, and the Holy Spirit. Jesus himself declared the Spirit would speak "only what he hears" (John 16:13); he brings us the message of the Father and the Son (vv. 14–15), who are in total agreement. The Spirit, then, is inviting us into the pure and undefiled truth of heaven. We are not receiving opinions or even practical wisdom but truth without additives or filler, straight from the author of truth himself.

How does the Spirit lead us into truth? He illuminates our minds as we read the Bible, giving us understanding and helping us apply what we read to our everyday lives. Scripture is the Word of God, a faithful and reliable guide for the life of faith. And when the Spirit speaks to us in the depths of our soul, he never contradicts the Bible, for he inspired every word. That means, for all who love the Lord, the Word and the Spirit are never in disagreement. Both offer us truth; both press us toward divine reality.

The author of Scripture lives inside of you. Listen for his voice. Devour his Word. Walk in truth each and every day.

Spirit of truth, awaken my mind, quicken my spirit, and open my heart to all that you have for me.

WHAT GOD WANTS

I have hidden your word in my heart
that I might not sin against you.

PSALM 119:11

In the ancient world, myriad gods competed for
the worship and allegiance of the masses. Personal
devotion to a single god was a rarity. Most people paid
homage to many gods to make sure every area of life
was covered. So, when Yahweh told the Israelites, "You
shall have no other gods before me" (Exodus 20:3),
it was a radical command. God didn't just want his
people to follow and obey him; he demanded they
forsake all other gods in order to be his special people.

Today, the situation is really no different. Myriad
gods compete for the hearts of men and women
around the globe, and many people hedge their bets
by offering themselves to many different gods. While
most of us don't keep idols on a shelf, we do worship
at the altars of wealth, security, comfort, and pleasure.
Our priorities reveal our false gods. And yet, Yahweh's
calling has not changed. To follow him, we must
forsake all other gods.

Loyalty. That's what God is after. He wants us
to delight ourselves in him (Psalm 37:4). He wants us
to be undivided in our allegiance (Ezekiel 11:19). He

wants us to offer our "bodies as a living sacrifice, holy and pleasing to God" (Romans 12:1). At baptism, we declare our allegiance to the one, true God and his Son, Jesus Christ (1 Peter 3:21). And every day after, we must hide his Word in our hearts, bringing it so deep that it becomes a part of us.

If God's thoughts take up space in our minds, we will begin to think like him. If God's passions and concerns occupy our hearts, we will love what he loves. Loyalty is lived not merely by sinning less (although that's a wonderful by-product) but also by becoming more like the God we serve and standing firm in this god-saturated world. In faithfulness to Yahweh, we declare what Scripture proclaims: that these gods never deliver on their promises; their way is the path to death, not life. The only route that brings us home is the one carved out by the Maker of every good thing.

God didn't wait for you to prove your loyalty to him. He revealed his commitment when he sent his Son to die for your sins. Your life has been given back to you so that you might walk in step with the God who loves you and experience life "to the full" (John 10:10).

God above all gods, I pledge my life to you. Shape my heart and renew my mind.

THE SPIRIT WALK

Moved by the Spirit,
he went into the temple courts.
LUKE 2:27

Have you ever had a divine appointment? Though you hadn't planned it, God brought you right where you needed to be to meet someone's need, or perhaps it was your need that was met. Either way, looking back, you can see God's fingerprints all over the situation. As we tune our spiritual ears to hear from the Spirit, we'll have more of these divine appointments. The Holy Spirit directs our steps all the time, but often we are too busy or too focused on earthly matters to notice.

Simeon had a divine appointment. Scripture tells us it wasn't his idea to enter the temple court the day he met Jesus. For all we know, he was planning on getting some shopping done downtown. Perhaps he had made plans to visit a friend. Whatever was on his morning calendar, he gave it up to follow the promptings of the Spirit. He was "moved" by God and headed to the temple courts, not quite knowing why. And there, amidst all the religious hustle and bustle, the Spirit directed his eyes toward a baby. We have no reason to believe Jesus looked anything but ordinary—just a typical six-week-old Jewish baby boy there in the temple with his parents, like so many others. But through the eyes of the Spirit, Simeon saw something else: the Messiah he had been waiting for his whole life.

The Spirit had told Simeon he would not die until he laid his eyes on the Promised One (v. 26). He was now advanced in years, but he had held on to that promise each and every day. And at last, he held hope in his arms. Reading Simeon's story in Luke 2, you can practically see the old man beaming from ear to ear. "Sovereign Lord, as you have promised, you may now dismiss your servant in peace. For my eyes have seen your salvation" (vv. 29–30).

Simeon was specially blessed because his time on earth collided with the earthly life of the Son of God, but he was not unique. You, too, were born again to be led by the Holy Spirit, to be moved out of your comfort zone and into position for God's kingdom purposes. You were made to have many divine appointments in your time. "For those who are led by the Spirit of God are the children of God" (Romans 8:14). Listen for his voice, and he will direct your steps.

Spirit of God, move me. I don't want to miss a single thing you have for me.

THE PUZZLE OF SCRIPTURE

None of the rulers of this age understood it, for if they had, they would not have crucified the Lord of glory.

1 CORINTHIANS 2:8

Have you ever read the Gospels and thought to yourself, *What's wrong with these people? How can they not know who Jesus is?*

Those of us who grew up in the church were trained to see Jesus all over the Old Testament. He's the serpent-crushing offspring foretold to Adam and Eve (Genesis 3:15). He's the blessing to all nations promised to Abraham (12:3). He's the true Passover Lamb (Exodus 12:6–7, 13). He's the King who will sit on David's throne forever (2 Samuel 7:12–13). He's the child who will be born of a virgin and called Immanuel, "God with us" (Isaiah 7:14). He's the Suffering Servant, by whose "wounds we are healed" (53:5).

Jesus himself taught his disciples to read the Old Testament this way (Luke 24:25–27). And yet, as he preached the kingdom of God and performed signs and wonders, very few people recognized him as the Savior God had promised. In fact, the religious leaders and those who spent their lives studying the Scriptures seemed to be the most certain that Jesus could not be the Messiah. How could they miss him?

In reality, the clues provided in the Old Testament are not so straightforward. Many of them do not speak directly of the Messiah (like the passage in Isaiah about the Suffering Servant); others had more than one fulfillment (like the child born of a "virgin," or "young woman" in Hebrew). Each prophecy and promise is like a puzzle piece, but the puzzle does not provide a complete picture of Jesus until all the pieces are in place. God did this because he knew it wouldn't only be his people reading the words of the Old Testament.

The rulers of this age—dark spiritual forces who would like nothing more than to stop the Messiah— knew God revealed his plans to his children, and so they searched for clues. But they did not understand that the way of salvation would come through death. In crucifying Jesus, they tried to destroy him, but in reality, they helped to secure the very redemption they wanted to thwart. God used their own predictable wickedness against them.

When you read the Bible, don't be worried if certain details don't make sense at first. The Holy Spirit will reveal the truth. Just hold on to what you know for certain and keep your eyes focused on the goodness of God.

God of all mysteries, I come to your Word with hunger and humility. Open my eyes to the truth.

THE BATTLE FOR HOLINESS

The mind governed by the flesh is death,
but the mind governed by the Spirit is life and peace.

ROMANS 8:6

Like a scary movie where the killer is calling from somewhere inside the house, our own flesh is out to destroy us. Born with a sinful nature, we come into this world with one foot already in the grave, alienated from God and robbed of the peace that was to be our birthright. Our minds are fixed on self-destructive pleasures, and none of us is strong enough to break the spell.

Simply put, "Those who are in the realm of the flesh cannot please God" (v. 8). But then Jesus came to sever the ties that hold us down. Through his death and resurrection, a new day dawned. Jesus' death paid the penalty for our sins, and his perfect righteousness brought us eternal life—and now the Holy Spirit is at work to make us holy and good, just like Jesus.

Those who belong to Christ have been transferred from the kingdom of darkness to the kingdom of God's Son (Colossians 1:13–14). That is where we find ourselves—as kingdom citizens living in step with the new age that has broken into the old. Our flesh still wants to destroy us, but now the Spirit of God is working within us. And so, we must choose each day whom we will serve—the evil deeds of the flesh or the righteousness of the Spirit.

This battle is waged on several fronts, but no stage is more critical than the mind. Before a person ever sins with their body, they make an agreement with their sinful nature in their minds. Therefore, every day—and throughout each day—we must give our thoughts over to the Spirit of God. Our minds must be continually renewed if we are ever to stand against our own flesh (Romans 12:2). By setting our minds on things above, we deprive our sinful nature of oxygen, and it atrophies.

Your marching orders may appear daunting at first, yet they are surprisingly simple: "Put to death the misdeeds of the body" (8:13), and in so doing, take hold of the life God has for you. Remember what Jesus has done on your behalf. Know that the same Spirit who raised him from the dead has now taken up residence in your mortal body to bring you life (v. 11). Rise up and walk with the Holy Spirit, for he is leading you in the footsteps of Jesus.

Righteous God, thank you for saving me. Help me now as I wage a battle for holiness in my life.

YOUR SECOND BIRTHRIGHT

The secret things belong to the LORD our God, but
the things revealed belong to us and to our children
forever, that we may follow all the words of this law.

DEUTERONOMY 29:29

The Bible is sufficient and complete, perfect and
good. A person could feast for a lifetime on the Word
of God and never go hungry. It's no wonder the
psalmist wrote, "The sum of your word is truth, and
every one of your righteous rules endures forever"
(Psalm 119:160 ESV). And yet, the Bible does not
answer all the questions we might like.

Most of Scripture is written in a succinct
manner, with many details and descriptions left to the
reader's imagination. There are spiritual mysteries the
Bible touches upon but never explores. For that matter,
the Bible is silent about most of Jesus' earthly life. But
none of this is by mistake. The Holy Spirit directed and
inspired precisely what he wanted us to have. When it
comes to the Word of God, we may be left wondering,
but we have not been left wanting.

No mere human being can explain why Scripture
speaks to certain things while not mentioning others at
all, but we do know that God is good, and we can rest

upon that fact. Nothing is missing from the Word of God. Every last jot and tittle the Lord intended are there.

The mysteries left untold—the "secret things"—belong to the Lord. He may speak to us of these things one day in glory, but for now, they are off-limits. However, that which he has revealed to us in the Bible is ours without reservation. God means for us to take hold of it, to internalize it, to live it, and to obey it fully. We are people who live by the Book. It is our privilege and our second birthright.

It would be fair to say there is no such thing as a believer who neglects the Word of the Lord. It would be like a fish that rejects the water or a bear that has given up on the outdoors. Scripture is our environment, for God has created us to live in the security of what he has spoken. It is faithful and true and brings light to shatter the darkness (see Genesis 1:3–5).

Your Father in heaven has given you the Bible, so don't shy away from it. Life and light and truth are on every page. Consider it your letter from home.

All-knowing God, pierce my heart and awaken my mind. Bring light to every dark corner of my life.

WHERE LIVING WATER FLOWS

On the last and greatest day of the festival,
Jesus stood and said in a loud voice,
"Let anyone who is thirsty come to me and drink."

JOHN 7:37

The Feast of Tabernacles commemorated the wilderness wanderings of the Israelites. Under Moses, the whole nation had lived in tents as they followed the angel of Yahweh for forty years before entering the promised land. God did not want his people to forget the lessons of that generation, so he commanded his people to come together and celebrate once a year (Leviticus 23:33–43).

As often happens with holidays, the traditions associated with Tabernacles grew as time passed. One important part of the celebration in Jesus' day was a reading from the book of Zechariah, which included this prophecy: "On that day living water will flow out from Jerusalem, half of it east to the Dead Sea and half of it west to the Mediterranean Sea, in summer and in winter" (Zechariah 14:8). The Jews believed God himself would one day rule from Jerusalem. Living water flowing east and west out of the city symbolized his global rule. As part of the festivities, priests would bring water from the nearby Pool of Siloam and pour it out at the base of the altar in the temple.

It was in this environment that Jesus stood up and said, "Whoever believes in me, as Scripture has said, rivers of living water will flow from within them" (John 7:38). The living water was supposed to flow from the city—from the throne of the Lord—but Jesus declared it would flow from people. This water is the Holy Spirit (v. 39), and he overflows from those who have put their faith in Jesus.

It would have been unimaginable to those gathered at the Feast of Tabernacles that day with Jesus, but God's Spirit is not bound to a building or a city; he now reigns from within his people. This water was given to us so that we would never thirst again (4:14), but it's also *living* water; it's supposed to flow out of us and into the world. The Spirit we carry in our brittle frames is meant to draw others into the kingdom so that, as Zechariah said, "The LORD will be king over the whole earth" (Zechariah 14:9).

You are a vessel of the Holy Spirit, and he is the living water the world desperately needs. Let his presence flow out of you until the whole earth is "filled with the knowledge of the glory of the LORD as the waters cover the sea" (Habakkuk 2:14).

King of kings, my heart is your throne. Let your goodness and mercy flow through me.

The Milk of the Word

Like newborn babies, crave pure spiritual milk,
so that by it you may grow up in your salvation.
1 Peter 2:2

If you've spent much time with newborns, you know they cry. A lot. Of course, their cries are not like the mind-splitting shrieks of a displeased toddler who merely wants his way. A newborn's siren is genuine. The little bundle is telling you he or she actually needs something. It could be a fresh diaper or a tightened swaddle, but more often than not, it's milk. These little ones eat around the clock, with each session normally lasting until they are ready to pass out from satisfaction.

If infants don't eat enough, they may begin to lose weight. And when you're starting out in the single digits, every ounce matters. As any pediatrician will tell you, regular and substantial feedings are incredibly important to a child's development. Without them, a baby cannot thrive. Babies need milk—and lots of it. Truthfully, so do we. Every follower of Jesus needs regular and substantial feedings on the milk of God's Word. Without ongoing meals from the Bible, we won't grow; we won't thrive. The apostle Peter says we ought to "crave" this milk. It ought to be our heart's cry morning, noon, and night.

Notice that Peter says the spiritual milk we are to crave must be "pure." That's because some teachers dilute the Word of God with their own viewpoints and prejudices. Others twist Scripture until their interpretation no longer speaks the heart of God. And still others disregard the Bible altogether in favor of man-made wisdom, new age babble, and spiritual-sounding mumbo jumbo—and they do it in the name of Jesus. These substitutes do not give life but rob it. They have nothing of substance in them to cause growth. In the moment, false teaching does little more than tickle itching ears (2 Timothy 4:3), but in the long run, it leads a person far from the Lord.

Make no mistake—you were once dead (Ephesians 2:1). But when you came to Christ, you were given new life. You are now born again (1 Peter 1:23). Just like a baby in the natural world, you must have milk to sustain your new life and to mature (Ephesians 4:14). But unlike that baby, you will never outgrow your need for the milk of God's Word.

Yahweh, my provider, whet my appetite so that my soul will not be satisfied by anything less than pure spiritual milk.

BABEL UNDONE

When they heard this sound, a crowd came together
in bewilderment, because each one heard their own
language being spoken.

ACTS 2:6

Exile from Eden is the sort of thing a person can never really get over. In fact, the hole left by paradise lost didn't just haunt Adam and Eve; it stayed in the collective memory of humanity for generations. If you listen carefully, you can still hear its echoes today.

It should come as no surprise, then, that just a few chapters into the book of Genesis, we see people trying to reclaim Eden on their own terms. When they started laying bricks for the Tower of Babel, the plan wasn't merely to build an impressive structure; it was to create "a tower that reaches to the heavens" (Genesis 11:4)—in other words, a place where heaven and earth come together, just like Eden. When God came down and saw what the people were doing, he confused their language, and they scattered to form the nations of the world, leaving the dream of a man-made way back to Eden unrealized.

Fast-forward several thousand years to Pentecost in Jerusalem, just a few weeks after Jesus died and rose again. On that day, the Holy Spirit descended on the house where many of Jesus' disciples had gathered. They began speaking in other languages, and Jews from the nations of the world who had come for the festival took notice. Peter addressed the crowd and explained what they were witnessing. Then he offered an invitation: "Repent and be baptized, every one of you, in the name of Jesus Christ for the forgiveness of your sins. And you will receive the gift of the Holy Spirit" (Acts 2:38).

God made a way back to Eden, and Jesus paid for it with his blood. The language confusion the people experienced at Babel had divided the world, but at Pentecost, the Spirit of the Lord brought another miracle of language, this time creating one new people of God from many nations.

It doesn't matter where you were born. It doesn't matter what language you speak. God has made a way for you to spend eternity with him in paradise. He did it all, and the blessing is yours by grace. The Holy Spirit brought your invitation at Pentecost, and once you accepted, he made his home with you. One day, heaven and earth will come together again (Revelation 21:10), just like in Eden—and you will be welcomed with open arms.

God of the nations, light a fire in my heart so that every day is like Pentecost.

MADE TO LAST

"The grass withers and the flowers fall,
but the word of our God endures forever."

ISAIAH 40:8

Life is short. It doesn't seem that way when you're a kid, though. When you're in grade school, age thirty seems so distant that it might as well be a million. But time is relentless. It plods on, day after day, year after year. Thirty comes and goes. Then forty and fifty, and before you know what's hit you, you realize you have fewer days ahead than behind. Eternity becomes visible out on the horizon. It's no wonder God compares us to grass (v. 6)—vibrant and green one day and dust on the wind the next.

Our lives aren't the only things that don't last. God also says our faithfulness is like the flowers of the field, sprouting up with promise only to come crashing back to earth in silent retreat (vv. 6–8). A quick read through the Scriptures or a look deep inside ourselves tells us this is true. We all sin, and we all break our promises to the Lord. It is his faithfulness—not ours—that keeps us standing. That is because "the word of our God endures forever." Not a single good promise or miraculous declaration that proceeds from the mouth of our Creator in heaven will fail.

Long before you were born, there was the Word of God. Long after you're gone, that same Word will be just as true, just as good, just as relevant as it is today. In a world that's constantly changing, the Bible needs no updating, no reimagining, and no revision. Every word is as beautiful and life-giving as the day it was written, and it loses no color as it ages. Scripture is a sure and steady rock on which to place our weight. It will stand when everything else fails (Matthew 24:35).

Of course, the Bible is more than declarations of truth and revelations of God's character. It is also an expression of love from our Father. The love of God lasts from eternity to eternity (Psalm 89:2). It's bigger and bolder than anything we can imagine, and it does not lose its potency with time. Though we are but grass, we have the privilege of discovering what it is to be the object of a love that lasts forever.

When you're weary and worn from life's disappointments, know that they will come to an end. But you were made for eternity. As you age, may the never-ending love of God shine all the brighter and become a beacon that points you home.

Voice of truth, thank you for your enduring Word. Use it in my life to prepare me for eternity.

ON THE DAY OF SMALL THINGS

He said to me, "This is the word of the LORD
to Zerubbabel: 'Not by might nor by power,
but by my Spirit,' says the LORD Almighty."

ZECHARIAH 4:6

When things don't come together as quickly as we'd like, it's easy to wallow in discouragement. Just ask the single young woman still waiting for her beloved to show up. Or check in with the aspiring songwriter playing for tips on the street corner, trying to make ends meet while his career is stalled. Solomon hit the nail on the head when he wrote, "Hope deferred makes the heart sick" (Proverbs 13:12).

For the people of Judah who had returned from exile in Babylon, life had stalled out. By something of a miracle unprecedented in world history, God had allowed the Jews to return to their homeland. Soon after arriving, they laid the foundation of the temple. But then, construction came to a standstill. The people faced fierce opposition, and the work stopped. The temple of the Lord was left as a footprint in the sand.

Years passed with no progress. It seemed as though the temple would never be finished. The dream of restoring God's house was all but dead. And then God spoke to the prophet Zechariah. He said that Zerubbabel, the governor of Judea and a descendant of King David, would complete what he started (Zechariah 4:9). The temple would rise in the Jerusalem skyline once more.

Such a promise must have seemed impossible to Zechariah. For nearly two decades, any attempt to continue construction had been thwarted. Everything he could see told him it was a day of small things, not great things. But God said, "Do not despise these small beginnings" (v. 10 NLT).

With the Lord, the smallest increases multiply. Success does not depend on our own strength, ability, or power. Instead, it is the Spirit of God at work that makes all the difference (v. 6). Indeed, Zechariah and the people of Judah saw the new temple dedicated to God. It happened because God had declared it, and his Spirit delivered it. "This house was finished on the third day of the month of Adar, in the sixth year of the reign of Darius the king" (Ezra 6:15 ESV).

It doesn't matter if the deck is stacked against you. It doesn't matter if you feel stuck in the waiting room on the day of small things. The Lord's plans for your life *will* come to pass. Hold tight. It's not by your striving but by the Spirit of God that his will is accomplished.

God who sees me, I surrender everything to you. Direct my life by your Spirit's power.

THE GIFT OF MUSIC

Let the message of Christ dwell among you richly as you teach and admonish one another with all wisdom through psalms, hymns, and songs from the Spirit, singing to God with gratitude in your hearts.

COLOSSIANS 3:16

Have you ever thought about how magical a thing music actually is? Notes and tones and keys arranged in an endless variety of combinations and tempos produce beautiful melodies that get stuck in our heads and hearts. Music is an avenue for worship, allowing us to enter the throne room of heaven and draw near to God (Psalm 100:4). It should come as no surprise, then, that the longest book in the Bible is a book of songs.

A world filled with music is evidence of God's goodness. Strictly speaking, no one needs music; very little in it is utilitarian. Rather, music is a bit of heaven's joy floating on the air, a gift from the Creator to his creation. Music is also powerful. Think about your favorite songs from way back. You can probably remember all the words. And just remembering the tunes may have even brought a smile to your face.

Is it any wonder, then, that the apostle Paul instructs believers to "teach and admonish one another with all wisdom through psalms, hymns, and songs from the Spirit"? If we want to be saturated with Scripture, wrapped up in the gospel, and walking in truth, we need a soundtrack to dance to. Yes, we should read, memorize, and study the Word of God, but we should also sing it to each other and to the Lord. Music is an express lane to our hearts. When we hear Scripture set to music—whether it's word-for-word or a creative arrangement of eternal truth—we take it in. If we listen long enough, it becomes part of us.

"Let the message of Christ dwell among you richly," wrote Paul. Bible scholars are divided on precisely what Paul meant by "the message of Christ." It may refer to the gospel about Jesus' life, death, and resurrection, or it might be a reference to his teachings. Regardless of what the good apostle intended with this verse, we can all agree that we ought to be people soaked in the gospel *and* the teachings of Jesus. And so, Paul's prescription—and our calling—includes music.

Let God's Word fill your ears. As you listen, allow his love to reach into your heart. Cultivate a life of worship and thanksgiving. "Sing to him a new song" (Psalm 33:3). The Christian life is set to music, and you've been invited to sing with the band.

O God, my strength and my song. Fill my heart with your good Word and set my feet dancing to its rhythm.

MARKED FOR GLORY

You also were included in Christ when you heard the message of truth, the gospel of your salvation. When you believed, you were marked in him with a seal, the promised Holy Spirit.

EPHESIANS 1:13

Whether it's a little girl scrawling her name on the tag of her favorite stuffed bear or a first-time home buyer whose name now graces a title deed, ownership matters. We want the things that are important to us to be ours, exclusively and officially. So does God. That is why he has marked every believer with a seal, his Holy Spirit.

In the ancient world, a king often had a signet ring. Pressing the ring into hot wax, he sealed official documents and decrees. His seal carried his authority, and people knew it. We see this sort of thing at work in the book of Daniel. After Daniel was lowered into the den of lions, "a stone was brought and placed over the mouth of the den, and the king sealed it with his own signet ring and with the rings of his nobles, so that Daniel's situation might not be changed" (Daniel 6:17). If anyone opened the den to rescue Daniel in the middle of the night, the broken seals would alert the authorities (see also Matthew 27:66). The seals also told the world that Daniel's sentence of death was sanctioned by the king; it was not to be questioned or overturned.

The Holy Spirit is God's official seal on your life. You are precious to him, and so he has marked you as his own, proclaiming to both the natural and supernatural worlds that your sins have been forgiven, your redemption is certain, and your inheritance is guaranteed (Ephesians 1:14). His mind is made up. His word is final.

Most of us know, instinctively, this doesn't make sense. We are flawed and broken, unworthy of heaven. We have all disobeyed the Lord's commands and chased after other gods. We have failed to reflect God's image to a watching world. To put it mildly, we are undeserving of the King's love. And yet, he does love us. He sent his Son to die in our place so that neither the power of death nor the devil himself could make a claim on us. And now that he has rescued us from the fire, he has put his Spirit within each of us.

The King has placed his seal on your life. Let it be a reminder of where you are headed and just how much it cost.

Redeemer of my wayward heart, hold me close to you and never let me go.

LIKE HEARING SCRIPTURE
FOR THE FIRST TIME

When the king heard the words of the Book of the
Law, he tore his robes.

2 KINGS 22:11

How did it happen? How is it possible that the people
of Judah, "entrusted with the oracles of God" (Romans
3:2 ESV), misplaced the Scriptures, or at least a sizeable
portion of them?

It's a strange and unexpected scene in the middle
of 2 Kings. King Josiah had just ordered repairs made
to the long-neglected temple of the Lord in Jerusalem.
At some point during the construction phase, Hilkiah
the high priest, or perhaps a worker reporting to him,
stumbled upon a scroll or series of scrolls. It's unclear
if "the Book of the Law" he found comprised the entire
five books of Moses or just Deuteronomy. Either way, it
was quite a find—a long-lost portion of God's Word.

The discovery of this book quite literally changed
the nation of Judah. Josiah was cut to the heart after
hearing the covenant read aloud. He knew instantly
that his people were guilty of great sin and idolatry
against Yahweh, so he brought everyone together and
renewed the covenant. Then, he initiated a series of
reforms designed to curb evil in the land: He removed

from the temple every object used for the worship of Baal, Asherah, or the stars in the sky (2 Kings 23:4). He also tore down the high places and altars to foreign gods throughout the country (v. 19), executed wicked priests for their treason against the one true God (v. 20), gave the boot to the mediums and spiritists living in the land, and tossed all the idols and household gods he could find (v. 24). He even reinstituted the celebration of Passover (v. 21). The Word of God penetrated Josiah's heart and inspired him to action. Very quickly, he became a man on a mission.

There's zero chance some forgotten bit of Scripture will be uncovered in our day. We have the Word of God, complete and whole. However, that doesn't mean we won't stumble upon something new as we read. Even if you've read the entire Bible cover to cover, don't be surprised if something you've never noticed before catches you by surprise.

Come to God's Word expecting to hear from the Lord. Open your heart, for the Creator of all things has bent low to meet with you. Be ready to be challenged. Be ready to be changed. And like Josiah before you, be ready to act.

God who speaks, reveal all the places in my life that need reformation and renewal.

LOVE IS THE REASON

If I have the gift of prophecy
and can fathom all mysteries and all knowledge,
and if I have a faith that can move mountains,
but do not have love, I am nothing.

1 CORINTHIANS 13:2

Is there anything sadder than people who've fought
and scraped and pulled themselves up on the ladder
of success only to discover that recognition and
wealth don't bring happiness? Money, on its own, is a
trap. Peace is not found at the bottom of a multipage
bank statement. Joy does not come from leadership
conferences and books. Hope cannot be purchased, no
matter how many connections a person has.

You see, gifts from God are not meant to stop
with the recipient. Every gift from God is meant to
flow through us, not just into us. God intends for
our money, time, and resources to bless others. The
same is true of the gifts of the Holy Spirit. Let's face it:
prophecy, words of knowledge, healing, and other sign
gifts are like spiritual superpowers God has placed into
jars of clay (see 2 Corinthians 4:7). And as jars of clay,
our job is to let his gifts overflow out of the jar and into
our brothers and sisters.

The apostle Paul wrote, "Everything must be done so that the church may be built up" (1 Corinthians 14:26). This is true not just of the overtly miraculous gifts but also of the gifts that sometimes fly under the radar—teaching, mercy, evangelism, and a slew of others. The Spirit has given them all that we might have another vehicle to love God and love one another.

It seems the Lord has always operated in this way. When he first called Abraham, he said, "I will make you into a great nation, and I will bless you;…and all peoples on earth will be blessed through you" (Genesis 12:2–3). Though Abraham's calling was unique in redemption history, God's strategy hasn't really changed. Every disciple of Jesus has been blessed to be a blessing.

In the New Testament, spiritual gifts are literally "gifts of grace." We don't deserve them, we can't earn them, and we cannot produce them on our own, no matter how hard we try. And yet God has given them so that we might be a blessing to others. Isn't that just like our heavenly Father? He has made us rich so that we can be generous with the people he has placed in our lives. What an incredible privilege!

Love is the reason Jesus called you to follow him, and love is the reason he has blessed you with spiritual gifts.

Generous God, as I learn to walk in the gifts you've given me, make me a vessel of your love.

THE SOWER'S WARNING

"Still other seed fell on good soil.
It came up and yielded a crop,
a hundred times more than was sown."
LUKE 8:8

Plants are persnickety. In order for our leafy green friends to grow from seed, everything needs to be just right. Whether you're dealing with tomatoes or gardenias, the temperature, the light, the soil, and the moisture all need to work together to create a hospitable environment. Then and only then will the little sprouts grow up to their full potential.

Farmers and gardeners know this, and so does Jesus. His parable of the sower is recorded in three of the four Gospels, so that may be a gentle nudge from the Holy Spirit to pay extra close attention. At first glance, the simple story reads like an agricultural allegory or farm-fresh riddle, but when we take Jesus' explanation into account, the parable takes on a darker hue. It's actually a warning to us all.

The seed that is sown "is the word of God" (v. 11), but just like for seeds in a garden bed, all the elements need to be just right in order for the word to germinate, grow to its full height, and produce its fruit. On the path, the seed is crushed underfoot and snatched up by birds. Like that hard path, a hard heart gives purchase to the devil, and he will rip the word away before it can ever be received (vv. 5, 12). On rocky ground, the seed grows, but its roots cannot burrow deep enough to find moisture, and so the plant withers and dies. Similarly, a heart that is shallow—that does not fully understand God's calling—will fail when tested and fall away (vv. 6, 13). Among the thorns, the seed grows but only until its life is squeezed out by the weeds. A heart that allows stresses and worldly distractions to remain will soon have no room for the word of God (vv. 7, 14).

In each case, there is absolutely nothing wrong with the seed. God's word is perfect and ready to take root; it just needs the good soil of a tender heart. Jesus' calling is clear: be ready for the word when it comes to you.

The Bible says, "Keep your heart with all vigilance, for from it flow the springs of life" (Proverbs 4:23 ESV). And within your heart, the Word of God— the Bible—is ready to take root. So let me ask you: How is your heart?

Sower of seed, show me where my heart has grown calloused and where weeds have sprouted up. Prepare me to receive your Word.

IMMERSED IN THE SPIRIT

"I baptize you with water for repentance.
But after me comes one who is more powerful than I,
whose sandals I am not worthy to carry.
He will baptize you with the Holy Spirit and fire."

MATTHEW 3:11

When John came preaching and baptizing in the Jordan River, it wasn't an entirely new spectacle. In fact, the Jews of the first century were well acquainted with baptism. There were stepped baths all over ancient Israel, and the people used them regularly to maintain ritual purity. Before a festival like Passover or Tabernacles, people would immerse themselves. Before entering the temple, people would immerse themselves.

Even so, John's baptism had a certain bite to it. It wasn't about restoring or maintaining any sort of outward, ritual purity. His was a baptism of repentance. He stood up in the wilderness and charged people from every walk of life to turn from their sin in preparation for the coming Messiah. John's baptism was all about internal, spiritual cleansing. And yet, even John knew there was a better baptism coming: "But after me comes one who is more powerful than I…He will baptize you with the Holy Spirit and fire."

As a race, we come into this world with hearts of stone (Ezekiel 11:19). We are unable to follow God as we should (Psalm 14:3). The baptism of the Holy Spirit, however, enables us to walk with him. Long before John donned his camel hair and shouted to the crowds with locusts on this breath, God made a promise to his people through the prophet Ezekiel: "I will give you a new heart and put a new spirit in you…And I will put my Spirit in you and move you to follow my decrees and be careful to keep my laws" (Ezekiel 36:26–27; see also Isaiah 44:3).

The baptism Jesus brought was not merely symbolic, as water baptism is; it also came with power (Acts 1:8). God's own Spirit floods Jesus' followers and makes them new. By walking in step with the Spirit, our lives can now produce the fruit of righteousness— "love, joy, peace," and all the rest (Galatians 5:22–25). Of course, the baptism of the Holy Spirit does not damage our free will. We must choose to live according to the Spirit's promptings and his convictions. But in the Spirit, we have become people who are now able to please God.

Never take for granted the Spirit of God living inside of you. Make the choice each day to move as he moves you, to walk where he guides you.

Spirit of love, make me sensitive to your leading. Make my life a pleasant aroma to God.

HOPE AND A FUTURE

No matter how many promises God has made,
they are "Yes" in Christ. And so through him
the "Amen" is spoken by us to the glory of God.

2 CORINTHIANS 1:20

Perhaps you know the verse. You may even have it
emblazoned on a T-shirt or coffee mug. It's Jeremiah
29:11, and it reads, "'For I know the plans I have for
you,' declares the LORD, 'plans to prosper you and not
to harm you, plans to give you hope and a future.'" It's
a promise from God that sounds almost too good to be
true. That's because, as many Bible readers will tell you,
it is. This verse is not for you, they'll say. It was part
of a letter Jeremiah sent to Jewish exiles in Babylon. It
was a divinely inspired word from the prophet to his
people—and it has nothing to do with you or me.

Except it does.

You see, God was telling the people of Judah that
their exile wouldn't last forever. One day—in seventy
years, to be precise (v. 10)—they would be allowed to
return home. Their sojourn in a foreign and wicked
nation would be over. They would be welcomed back
into the promised land. And true to his word, when
the time was completed, God permitted his people to
return to Judah.

While God's promises are always good, more often than not, they are bigger than they first appear— and they are all ours in Christ. Jesus is a better Savior than we could have imagined. You may not be able to trace your lineage back to ancient Judah, but you have been brought into God's family by the blood of his Son. Jeremiah 29:11, then, is part of your history—a marker of God's faithfulness on your journey. Not only that, but you are now part of a bigger and more glorious return from captivity.

Just like the Jews in Babylon, you are in exile, living here in this cursed world for just a little while longer. Soon, Jesus will return, and God will make all things new (Revelation 21:5). When he does, every heartache you've ever known will be wiped away, and you will be ushered into the promised land that endures forever, "a better country—a heavenly one" (Hebrews 11:16).

So, yes, wear Jeremiah 29:11 on a T-shirt proudly. God does indeed know the plans he has for you, "plans to give you hope and a future."

Alpha and Omega, help me to remember that while sometimes your promises are too good for me to fully understand, they are not too good to be true.

TILL THE LAST DAY

Now we see only a reflection as in a mirror;
then we shall see face to face. Now I know in part;
then I shall know fully, even as I am fully known.

1 CORINTHIANS 13:12

In many corners of the global church, a diabolical rumor has been circulating for centuries, weaving and winding its way into the hearts and minds of God's people, deceiving them into believing that God's power has all but retreated from this world. Brothers and sisters who accept this rumor may say they believe in miracles, healings, and the occasional divine intervention—they don't want to put God in a box, after all—but they don't expect God to give supernatural gifts to his children. They believe the sign gifts, described in the New Testament as commonplace in the first-century church, have ceased.

However, no matter how many intricate theological grids are placed over it, and no matter how its words are twisted, the Bible does not provide quarter for this abominable rumor. There is no indication in Scripture that the gifts of prophecy, tongues, healings, and the like would come to an abrupt end, either with the close of the apostolic generation or with the completion of the New Testament. Instead, God intended spiritual gifts of all sorts to be a part of the everyday Christian experience for the duration.

Paul told the Corinthian believers, "Eagerly desire gifts of the Spirit, especially prophecy" (1 Corinthians 14:1). That's a strange command to give to ordinary believers (who had a track record of abusing spiritual gifts) if the gifts were only intended to prove the authority of the apostles, as some have suggested, or if the gifts were going to fizzle out in a few short decades.

The apostle Paul actually said the gifts would not cease until "completeness comes" (13:10) or, to put it another way, until "the perfect comes" (ESV). What is this "completeness," this perfect state of being? It will come when we see Jesus, our returning Savior, face-to-face. Simply put, "the perfect" is life with Jesus in a renewed heaven and earth. Could there be anything more complete than that? All else leaves us wanting, with hope and longing lodged firmly in our hearts, for nothing this side of that glorious redemption moment will satisfy us fully.

Presbyterian or Pentecostal, Baptist or Brethren, God has invited you to knock on heaven's door and seek the gifts of his Holy Spirit. So, what are you waiting for? The time is now.

Gracious Father, I want everything you have for me. Use me as an instrument of your mercy and love.

HUMBLE ENOUGH TO BE WRONG

He began to speak boldly in the synagogue.
When Priscilla and Aquila heard him,
they invited him to their home and explained to him
the way of God more adequately.

ACTS 18:26

Here in the West, we are fixated on our jobs. Go to a dinner party or an after-church newcomers' luncheon—anywhere you'll be mixing with new people—and you can be certain that, more than once, you'll hear the question, "So, what do you do for a living?"

In our dual quests to climb the corporate ladder and keep up with the Joneses, we've allowed our jobs to define us. Along with that, we've become awfully protective of our turf. No one likes to be told how to do their job, especially by someone outside of their field. Most of us receive that sort of feedback as a challenge to our authority and identity.

As believers, we've been shown that our identity can't be tied to a job or a degree. Rather, our whole life—who we are, why we're here, and where we're headed—is bound up in Christ (Colossians 3:4). That is the truth, and it's positively wonderful. But there is one danger to look out for. If we're not careful, we can hold on to our particular theological tradition as though *that* were our identity rather than Jesus, and we will miss out on something good and beautiful.

In the book of Acts, we have the example of Apollos, a gifted preacher whose understanding of the gospel needed some work. Rather than playing the part of a professional Christian uninterested in contrary viewpoints, he graciously received correction from Priscilla and Aquila. In other words, he changed his doctrine when his new friends showed him truth from God's Word he hadn't considered properly before.

In essential matters—the person and work of Jesus, the authority of the Scriptures, and the way of salvation, to name a few key issues—hold tight. In the nonessentials, be gracious to listen to others, ready to test everything against the Bible, and willing to change if needed. Especially when it comes to passages of God's Word that are notoriously difficult to understand, be willing to explore new perspectives. The Bible is unfailing, but that doesn't always mean our initial understanding of it always will be.

Remember: your identity is in Christ, not in your church tradition or theological comfort zone. Seek God and seek his truth, no matter what. Apollos was the better for it, and so will you be.

Spirit of Jesus, make me humble to accept correction and eager to embrace the truth.

THE FRUIT THAT CHANGES YOU

The fruit of the Spirit is love, joy, peace.
GALATIANS 5:22

Miracle fruit is a special little berry from West Africa that earned its name because it has the unusual power to turn sour foods sweet. That's right—eat some miracle fruit and then take a big, bold bite out of a lemon. It won't bite back. Or take a generous swig of apple cider vinegar. You'll find it's become as pleasant as sweet tea. Of course, the miracle fruit does nothing to change the lemon or the vinegar; instead, it temporarily changes a person's taste receptors.

It's amazing how different the world can taste when we're changed on the inside. People filled with love, joy, and peace no longer need to purse their lips when confronted with the bitterness of this world. When Paul set out to describe the life of a Spirit-led Christian, he wrote of a fruit more magical than miracle fruit—the fruit of the Spirit that expresses itself in nine glorious virtues, the first three of which reveal how a believer is changed on the inside.

Love gives us a heart like the Lord's, for "God is love" (1 John 4:8). It shapes the way we look at other people—friends and enemies alike. As the Spirit works in us, the raging sea of prejudice, jealousy, and selfish ambition is made placid. Love brings us into alignment with God's commands (Galatians 5:14). "Love does not delight in evil but rejoices with the truth" (1 Corinthians 13:6). Love tunes our hearts to follow the Lord.

Joy is almost too good to be true. While the world chases after happiness—that good feeling that comes when our circumstances align with our personal preferences and desires—joy invites us to sing, no matter what season we're living through. It's no wonder the Old Testament declares, "The joy of the LORD is your strength" (Nehemiah 8:10).

Then there's peace. While Paul wrote to the Galatians in Greek, there can be little doubt that his Hebrew mind was thinking the whole time of *shalom*—the wholeness and deep prosperity the priests would speak over the people of Israel (Numbers 6:26). This is the supernatural "peace of God, which transcends all understanding," guarding our hearts and minds (Philippians 4:7). It is a precious gift in a world that seems to fall further into chaos with each passing day.

Follow the Spirit's leading. Walk in step with his rhythm. Soon, you'll find you're filled with love that wasn't there before, joy that lifts you up when others are brought low, and peace more powerful than any storm.

Jesus, true Vine, you are the source of every good thing in my life. Bear much fruit in me.

OBEY ANYWAY

Simon answered, "Master, we've worked hard all
night and haven't caught anything. But because you
say so, I will let down the nets."

LUKE 5:5

Being a commercial fisherman has never been easy.
It takes a certain type of person with a certain mental
and physical ruggedness to endure the long hours, the
dangerous conditions, and the uncertainty of it all. The
work itself is often grueling and exhausting, and open
water can be harsh and unforgiving. So it should come
as no surprise that most fishermen aren't looking for
tips and strategies from landlubbers. This was true in
the ancient world just as it is today.

Simon Peter had just spent the entire night out on
the water with nothing to show for his troubles. He knew
the Sea of Galilee better than most, and yet even he had
not been able to find where the fish were all hiding. The
only consolation was that it was over. Once his nets were
cleaned, he was going to head home and go to bed.

But then something happened: Jesus of Nazareth
got into his boat.

As Peter finished resetting the nets for another
evening, Jesus turned to him and asked him to push the
boat out a little ways; the acoustics off the water would

allow the large crowd on the shore to hear his message. It was a small thing, so Peter obliged. But when it was all over, Jesus made another request of Peter: "Put out into deep water, and let down the nets for a catch" (v. 4).

Fishing was Peter's domain, his world. He knew the time for a decent catch was over; the sun had risen, and the water was too warm for fish to congregate near the surface. But here's the remarkable thing: Peter agreed.

Even though Jesus' instructions didn't make any sense, even though they went against the grain of everything Peter knew about fishing, Peter listened to the Lord: "But *because you say so*, I will let down the nets" (emphasis added). The rest is fish-filled, miraculous history: the catch was so large the "nets began to break" (v. 6).

As you read the Bible, emulate Peter. Decide in the moment that you will obey the Lord's commands, whether or not they make much sense to you. "Love your enemies" (Matthew 5:44) may run afoul of this world's ethics; do it anyway. "Give thanks in all circumstances" (1 Thessalonians 5:18) may go against everything you feel in the midst of life's disappointments; do it regardless. We are to be the sort of people who respond to God, "Because you say so, I will obey."

Faithful One, thank you for guiding my steps. I want to obey simply because of who you are.

THE FRUIT THAT BLESSES OTHERS

The fruit of the Spirit is…
forbearance, kindness, goodness.

GALATIANS 5:22

What would you think of an apple tree that kept all of its fruit for itself? Imagine spying a delicious red-golden apple dangling from a leafy branch. You reach up, take hold, and pull, but the sucker won't budge. No matter how hard you try, you can't tear the apple from its stem, which is firmly and irrevocably connected to its bough.

Of course, this is nonsense. An apple tree—or any fruit tree, for that matter—would be useless (and ridiculous) if it couldn't share its fruit. The same is true of a Spirit-filled Christian. The fruit that comes from walking with the Holy Spirit is meant to be a blessing to others. It doesn't just change us on the inside; it needs to touch the world as well. In particular, our supernatural forbearance, kindness, and goodness are meant to bless others.

Forbearance typifies a person who has a long fuse and is not easily provoked. Such a believer is patient and restrained when injured or mocked. Out of the wellspring of love in her heart, she does not retaliate. No one modeled this behavior better than Jesus. "When they hurled their insults at him, he did not retaliate; when he suffered, he made no threats. Instead, he entrusted himself to him who judges justly" (1 Peter 2:23). That last bit is important—forbearance doesn't mean being a pushover or forgetting about justice; rather it means looking to God as the ultimate judge of human behavior.

Kindness and goodness are related as both radiate God's heart toward sinners. To be kind is to be warm and welcoming. To be good is to be morally pure, seeking the well-being of others. Kind people are unusually compassionate; they are sympathetic to the varied plights of those around them.

God, in his goodness, extends kindness to the lost and broken. He does this so that, in response, some might choose the path of repentance (Romans 2:4). It can be hard to fathom: God, the Creator and King of the universe, delivers kindness to those who seek to live as though he were dead, and he does it so that these enemies might receive an inheritance greater than all the treasures in the world.

Always remember: the spiritual fruit in your life—your forbearance, your kindness, your goodness—may be an avenue by which God reaches someone who does not yet know him. One of the reasons you have been blessed is so that others might be blessed through you.

God of abundance, as I walk in step with your Spirit, may others see your heart in me.

ON EATING WELL

When your words came, I ate them;
they were my joy and my heart's delight,
for I bear your name, LORD God Almighty.

JEREMIAH 15:16

Y ou've probably heard it said, "You are what you eat."
Barring any underlying medical issues, it's generally
true that if you eat healthful foods, you will be healthy.
That's because what you eat is more than fuel that is
spent as you live your life. Instead, the food you put
into your body becomes part of you. Over a long
period of time, it shapes your life and well-being.

Needless to say, it's vital to eat foods that are
good for you. Such is even more important when we
consider our spiritual diets. The prophet Jeremiah
knew this. When God's words came to him, he
devoured them as a meal so that they would become
part of him. As a prophet of Yahweh, he was a
representative of heaven. When speaking the words
of the Lord, Jeremiah's messages carried as much
weight as if the clouds had parted and God's voice had
thundered directly to the people. And if the citizens of
Judah were going to observe Jeremiah as God's man
here on earth, he wanted to make sure he was living in

sync with the heart of the Lord. Therefore, he eagerly ate the words of God as they came.

Jeremiah's ministry may have been unique, but you and I also represent God in our communities "as though God were making his appeal through us" (2 Corinthians 5:20). And so, just like Jeremiah, we need a steady diet of spiritual food from the Word of God. We need God's heart and God's holiness to become part of us—to change and shape how we live, how we speak, and how we love. The junk food of the world simply will not do.

A person who has survived on a diet of fast food, processed frozen dinners, and sugary snacks will find an adjustment to lean proteins, rich grains, and fresh vegetables a shock to his system. So will a person who has been dining on the spiritual equivalent—worldly philosophies, new age nonsense, and wisdom devoid of God. But there is good news. Just as, in time, the former junk-food junkie will begin craving wholesome meals, so, too, will the believer who has finally decided to stop neglecting the Bible. God's Word will become a "joy" and her "heart's delight" (Jeremiah 15:16).

With Scripture, God has laid out an extraordinary spread, a table filled with food as nutritious as it is delicious. It's all for you, and it's time to eat.

Compassionate Lord, thank you for feeding my spirit. Make me truly hungry for more of your Word.

THE FRUIT THAT WORSHIPS GOD

The fruit of the Spirit is…
faithfulness, gentleness and self-control.
GALATIANS 5:22–23

What comes to your mind when you think of worship? Hands and voices lifted high? A well-worn hymnal? A praise band with energy to spare? The apostle Paul wrote, "I urge you, brothers and sisters, in view of God's mercy, to offer your bodies as a living sacrifice, holy and pleasing to God—this is your true and proper worship" (Romans 12:1). So, while a life of worship includes singing praises to God, it must be bigger than that.

We believers were made to worship God, and honestly, it's the only proper response when confronted with who he is and what he's done for us. It should come as no surprise, then, that walking in the Spirit cultivates the fruit of worship in our lives— faithfulness, gentleness, and self-control.

Being faithful to God means believing him, trusting him, and leaning on him, no matter what. Faith in the Lord is essential because "without faith it is impossible to please God" (Hebrews 11:6). A life of faith is a declaration that God is more powerful than anything that might come against us, that he is more valuable than anything this world has to offer, and that he always keeps his promises.

Faith leads to gentleness because a gentle person does not insist on getting his way but, instead, defers to the Lord and his perfect plan. Think of Christ in Gethsemane, who, though anguished, prayed, "My Father, if it is possible, may this cup be taken from me. Yet not as I will, but as you will" (Matthew 26:39). Although we may not always understand God's ways, we know they are always higher than ours (Isaiah 55:9), and so we can give ourselves to the Lord gently and without reservation.

Finally, there is self-control. As we follow the leading of the Holy Spirit, we gain the strength to resist the urges and demands of our flesh and instead learn to follow the instructions of the Lord. In the Old Testament, God promised a day would come when the Spirit of God would empower his people to obey his commands (Ezekiel 36:27). He made good on that promise at Pentecost, but we must take hold of it by walking in step with his Spirit.

God sent the Holy Spirit into your life so that you might bear fruit for him. And the best part? There's no striving or fierce determination required. Just let the Spirit do his work and try to keep up!

Spirit of holiness, I yield my life to you as a living, breathing act of worship.

THE TIE THAT BINDS

"My prayer is not for them alone. I pray also for those
who will believe in me through their message,
that all of them may be one, Father, just as you
are in me and I am in you."

JOHN 17:20–21

There's a song from the 1960s, written by Peter
Scholtes, called "They'll Know We Are Christians by
Our Love," but all too often, the world sees something
else: the way we pull away from one another.
Thousands of church denominations exist worldwide,
and there are myriad opinions on nearly every topic
related to theology. Folks on one end of the spectrum
question the faith of their brothers and sisters on the
other end. They draw lines. They encircle their camps.
And on and on it goes.

While this division and self-segregation is
nothing new, it is foreign to the family of faith Jesus
breathed life into. His prayer, on the night he was
betrayed, included this desire for us: "that all of them
may be one, Father, just as you are in me and I am in
you." We have no reason to think Jesus changed his
mind on the subject; God the Son wants us to be as
close with one another as he is with the Father—and
nothing is closer than that!

So, how do we "reach unity in the faith and in the knowledge of the Son of God" (Ephesians 4:13) when there is so much that divides us? The answer lies in God's Word, or rather, the answer is God's Word. We're all reading the same psalms and stories. We're all studying the same messages and miracles. Even when we disagree on how to understand a particular passage or apply a certain teaching, we should be able to come together around the fact that we believe the Bible is truth, the very Word of God, and that in its pages the Lord reveals himself to us.

And there's more to it than that.

If we study Scripture on its own terms rather than through a theological grid with which we've grown comfortable, we'll discover rich truths. The more we understand, the more we'll find we have in common with Christians from other traditions who've chosen to approach Scripture the same way. Even where we disagree, our study will reveal to us just how difficult interpreting the Bible can sometimes be, and that will give us grace for our friends on the other side of the debate.

Hold fast to the Word of God. Dig deep and work to find common ground with other believers there, in the pages of Scripture.

Sun of Righteousness, as I study your Word, draw me closer to you and closer to my brothers and sisters.

SPIRIT POWER

"You will receive power when the Holy Spirit comes on you; and you will be my witnesses in Jerusalem, and in all Judea and Samaria, and to the ends of the earth."

ACTS 1:8

As a group, the disciples of Jesus weren't exactly brave. When soldiers arrested Jesus in the garden of Gethsemane, "all the disciples deserted him and fled" (Matthew 26:56). Peter, who was the leader of the pack, was so terrified of what the authorities might do to him that he denied knowing Jesus three times (vv. 69–75). And with the possible exception of John, none of the disciples were at the cross as Jesus suffered unimaginable agony. They were all too afraid and stayed away.

But then something happened—something that transformed this group of cowards into the greatest missionary force the world has ever seen. Certainly, seeing the resurrected Jesus with their own eyes had something to do with it, but there was something else: on the day of Pentecost, they were filled with the Holy Spirit and received power from God. This Holy Spirit's power made them bold and unashamed. They were willing to give up everything, including their lives, for the sake of the gospel.

You see, walking around with God in your chest has a way of making a person see the world differently. Learning to hear the Spirit's voice, and thus the heart of God, shapes a believer's priorities and silences her inhibitions. Experiencing the truth that nothing can separate you from God's love—"neither death nor life, neither angels nor demons, neither the present nor the future, nor any powers, neither height nor depth, nor anything else in all creation" (Romans 8:38–39)—has a way of driving out earthly fears.

But it wasn't just a lack of fear that drove Peter and the others to tell the ancient world about Jesus. It was the Spirit himself. The Holy Spirit is not at odds with the Father or the Son; he wants what they want: "all people to be saved and to come to a knowledge of the truth" (1 Timothy 2:4). And so, the Spirit is the greatest evangelist of all time. He is working through God's people—you and me included—to finish the task Jesus gave us (Matthew 28:18–20).

As you learn to hear the Spirit's voice and respond to his promptings, don't be surprised if he places you in situations where people need to hear the gospel. Don't be shy. You've received power from heaven—the presence of God living within you—to be a bold witness for Jesus.

Waymaker, you found me when I was lost. Now use me to find others.

BUILT ON THE ROCK

"Therefore everyone who hears these words of mine
and puts them into practice is like a wise man who
built his house on the rock."

MATTHEW 7:24

Anyone who's ever built a new home knows how
important it is to have a strong foundation. Though the
underpinnings of the building remain largely unseen,
they make all the difference. The house itself may be
well-built, richly appointed, and inviting, but without
the right footing, it will someday collapse into a heap of
used lumber.

In the Sermon on the Mount (Matthew 5–7),
Jesus gave his disciples and the gathered crowds a new
and solid foundation on which to build. He taught
them—and us—how to live in a way that reflects God's
good heart and his call to holiness and love. Then, he
gave a promise and issued a corresponding warning:
those who build their life on these words will have a
solid foundation to withstand the strongest of storms,
but those who hear these teachings and do not build
upon them will be washed away when the tempest
arrives (7:24–27).

Jesus' teaching about storms and rocks and sand
has to do with the Sermon on the Mount specifically,

but the same principle holds true when we consider all of Scripture: "As for God, his way is perfect: The LORD's word is flawless" (Psalm 18:30). Just remember: a solid foundation doesn't help a thing if you never build on it.

It's not enough to read the Bible. It's not enough to understand its basic teachings and nod in agreement. To build upon the Bible is to take it in and then live it out; it's to become a true disciple of Jesus, not just a fan or an admirer. As Jesus' half brother James wrote, "Do not merely listen to the word, and so deceive yourselves. Do what it says" (James 1:22).

Too often today, we see prominent and well-known Christians walking away from the faith or admitting to some deep-seated pattern of sin. Many of these folks love the Bible. They can quote it and teach it. They just never built a life upon it; they built upon shifting sand instead. Oh, the house they made was beautiful; it just wasn't built to last.

Your foundation matters. How you understand the God who loves you, the nature of your sin, and the world in which you live is of utmost importance. But once you know you're starting with the right foundation, go ahead and build something glorious.

Jesus, precious cornerstone, show me where my foundation needs repair. I want to build a life that honors you.

HOLY FIRE

Do not quench the Spirit.
1 THESSALONIANS 5:19

If you're not used to hearing other Christians speak in tongues, it can be unsettling. Likewise, if you don't spend much time around those who practice healing prayer, speak words of knowledge, or prophesy, those experiences may leave you scratching your head. They might even make you a bit uncomfortable. That's the way it can be with fire, especially when you're not used to it.

The Spirit of God is a holy fire, the very presence of Yahweh within us and within our midst. During the exodus, the presence of God was visible by fire at night (Numbers 9:15), and before that, the Lord made himself known to Moses through a burning bush (Exodus 3:2). Now, the Spirit of the Lord is a fire that burns whenever we come together. That is why Paul used language normally reserved for talk of fire when he warned, "Do not *quench* the Spirit" (emphasis added). We must be careful not to do anything that might curtail or suppress the fire of God.

When we gather as the family of faith, there certainly should be order (see 1 Corinthians 14:40), but it may be that some of us have grown so comfortable with our culture's version of order that we've squeezed out and pushed aside the Holy Spirit. Any time we neglect the Spirit or seek to limit his activity, we're out of bounds. It is God who should lead and we who should follow. We are supposed to wait upon him, not the other way around.

Oftentimes, as we open our worship services in prayer, we welcome God, but does our program make time for what he might want to do in our midst? We pray and ask the Lord to give us wisdom whenever we have an important decision to make, but are we too busy to sit and listen and wait for his answer? We may say we believe all the gifts of the Spirit are in operation today, but when we come together, do we really expect to see the Holy Spirit move among us? When it comes to the Spirit of God, our theology may be sound—perfectly in line with the teachings of Scripture—but if our hearts are not open to him, we have missed something critical.

Open yourself up. Surrender your emotions, your inhibitions, and your need to be in control. Invite the Holy Spirit to move in you—and really mean it. Kindle the flame already burning inside of you.

Holy fire of God, forgive me for the times when I have taken you for granted. I welcome you, here and now. I open my life to you without reservation.

THE OLD TESTAMENT MADE NEW

These things happened to them as examples and were written down as warnings for us, on whom the culmination of the ages has come.

1 CORINTHIANS 10:11

You may have heard that we Christians need to distance ourselves from the Old Testament. It's difficult not to notice how much bad press those thirty-nine books get these days—all of the conquests and animal sacrifices and patriarchal baggage. So, naturally, we might feel a temptation to skip past all that stuff and get to the New Testament and to Jesus.

Not so fast.

It's true: we live worlds apart from the various cultures of the ancient Near East. So, it's understandable that much of what we read in the Old Testament seems a bit strange and, in some cases, even offensive. But that's only because God steps into time and space as it exists, not as we'd like it to be. The Old Testament is the story of the God who draws near, the God who speaks our language, the God who reveals eternal truths using pictures and symbols we know. Every time God came close in the Old Testament, he was setting the stage for the day when Jesus would put on flesh and become one of us.

But the Old Testament isn't merely background material for the coming of Christ. God gave us the stories of everyone from Adam to Zechariah so that we might learn from them (Romans 15:4). Lest we imagine we are somehow immune from sin and the snares of the devil, we would do well to pay attention. Accounts of their struggles and failures were written down for us so that we might avoid the same traps (1 Corinthians 10:6, 11).

Beyond that, many events in the Old Testament point to deeper spiritual realities. For example, God rescued the Hebrew people from slavery in Egypt, and after a long sojourn in the wilderness, where he tested them and where they learned to follow the Lord, he delivered them to the promised land of Canaan. God also rescued us from slavery to sin, and we are now following God through the wilderness of this world as we await our entrance into the ultimate promised land, the city of God come to earth (Hebrews 13:14; Revelation 21:2). And so, it seems we have much in common with those who have gone before us. Perhaps our lives are not as different as we first imagined.

All of God's Word is for you. Every passage is there to help you as you take your place in the grand story of redemption.

Lion of Judah, give me insight into the deep truths hidden in your Word. Strengthen my walk with you.

THOSE WHO CARRY HIS LOVE

Hope does not put us to shame, because God's love
has been poured out into our hearts through the
Holy Spirit, who has been given to us.

ROMANS 5:5

The 1994 film *The Shawshank Redemption* takes place
almost entirely inside a prison. Murderers, thieves,
rapists, and the like are all locked up together behind
cold, gray walls, kept under the thumb of a crooked
and vicious warden. It's not exactly a setting for a feel-
good movie. And yet, the unrelenting theme of the film
is hope.

At one point, early on in the film, Ellis Boyd
"Red" Redding, played by Morgan Freeman, warns Tim
Robbins's Andy Dufresne: "Let me tell you something,
my friend. Hope is a dangerous thing. Hope can drive
a man insane."[1] Red is exactly right. Hope that is
based on nothing more than wishful thinking is very
dangerous. It can torment a soul already in pain. That
is why the gospel is such good news. It is the only sure
and perfect promise we can hold on to in this world.
No matter how dark things may seem, God will not
disappoint those who trust in him. Even so, the Lord,

---

1   *The Shawshank Redemption*, directed by Frank Darabont
(1994; Los Angeles, CA: Columbia Pictures, 1999), DVD, 142 min.

in his goodness, has given us a glorious taste of the final glory our hope is fixed on, here and now.

The Holy Spirit within us is our constant connection to the love of God. In times of despair and heartache, the Spirit whispers God's love to us. When pain and persecution come, the Spirit tells us again that God's love is bigger than any suffering we might bear in this life. As believers, we carry around the love of God. As we learn to listen to the promptings of the Spirit, that eternal and unchanging love will be our strength.

The Spirit's very presence is a reminder that the battle has been won. Jesus died to end the curse of sin, to remove death's sting, to crush the head of the devil. The fact that God's Spirit has taken up residence within our hearts is proof that we have been justified by Christ's sacrifice. We have been made new, transformed into walking, talking temples of the living God (1 Corinthians 6:19). And God set this all in motion "while we were still sinners" (Romans 5:8). If that isn't love, I don't know what is.

You are loved more than you know. Let God's love, which he has poured into you through the Holy Spirit, keep your hope alive. Jesus is coming back soon.

Father of love, help me to walk as the beloved child of the King that I am.

THE SECRET TO A BLESSED LIFE

Blessed is the one who does not walk in step with the wicked or stand in the way that sinners take or sit in the company of mockers, but whose delight is in the law of the LORD, and who meditates on his law day and night.

PSALM 1:1–2

At first, it might seem a strange thing to delight in the law of God. I don't know too many people who get excited about avoiding shellfish (Leviticus 11:10), making restitution for gored animals (Exodus 21:35–36), or reviewing detailed tent-building instructions (Exodus 26).

I'm more likely to flip to another part of Scripture to find my delight. It feels good to know God rejoices over his people with singing (Zephaniah 3:17), and it's an encouragement to hear that nothing in life or death can separate us from the love of God (Romans 8:38–39). I don't think I'm alone when I say it's not usually the commandments I long for when I need a shot of delight. And yet, the Psalter opens by telling us that those who find joy in God's many instructions are blessed.

Though some of the commandments in the law seem strange to us today—I'm looking in your direction, Deuteronomy 22:11—each one was given to the people of Israel for a reason. In fact, some of the fun of studying Scripture is digging in and uncovering what God was really teaching his people with these law codes. Beyond that, though, the commandments were a window into the heart of God.

God gave rules and instructions to his people in order to shape their character. His desire was—and still is—that they be holy, just as he is holy (Leviticus 11:44). This shouldn't come as a surprise. God created us to be holy (and good and just and faithful and playful and a thousand other things) just like him; that's why we're called his image-bearers (Genesis 1:27). The commandments of Scripture, then, are the path back home, the way back to our true humanity.

In speaking about the law, Jesus said, "Love the Lord your God with all your heart and with all your soul and with all your mind" (Matthew 22:37; compare with Deuteronomy 6:5), and "Love your neighbor as yourself" (Matthew 22:39; compare with Leviticus 19:18). Then he said, "All the Law and the Prophets hang on these two commandments" (Matthew 22:40).

There lies the secret to a blessed life: you will find tremendous delight when you forget yourself and spend your days loving God and loving others. That's what the law is all about, and it's what you were made for.

Righteous One, I want the joy of walking in your footsteps. Teach me your ways.

THE FATHER'S ARMS

Because you are his sons,
God sent the Spirit of his Son into our hearts,
the Spirit who calls out, "Abba, Father."

GALATIANS 4:6

Small children know they can climb up on Daddy's lap, no matter what. It doesn't matter if Dad is eating dinner, talking with friends, or taking part in a meeting; they have access to Daddy like no one else. They also know Dad is the one to see when something is wrong. Skinned knee? Run to Dad. Feeling sick? Climb up on Dad and take a nap. Can't get that little plastic straw into the juice box? Bring it to Dad.

Jesus knew what it was to lean on his Dad. Throughout his earthly life, he kept in constant contact with the Father, and in his most painful moments, he cried out to him as a beloved Son. On the night before his death, Jesus went to the garden of Gethsemane to pray. "'Abba, Father,' he said, 'everything is possible for you. Take this cup from me. Yet not what I will, but what you will'" (Mark 14:36). In his anguish, Jesus knew just where to turn.

The religious leaders of the day weren't too keen on Jesus referring to God as his very own Father. At one point, they tried to kill him for it (John 5:18). God had been the nation of Israel's Father (Deuteronomy 32:6; Isaiah 64:8), but no devout Jew would have dared to relate to God with such boldness and familiarity. Jesus, however, lived in the love he shared with his Father, and he told his disciples to live in that same love—God was their father too (John 20:17).

In Christ, we have been adopted as God's sons and daughters. But because we are prone to forget our place as children of the King, prone to forget that we can run to our Abba whenever we want, we have the Spirit of the Son—the Spirit of Jesus—inside of us (Galatians 4:6). We can pray with confidence, knowing that our Father hears us (1 John 5:14), cares for us (1 Peter 5:7), and will do whatever is necessary to bring about good for us (Romans 8:28).

Because of the Holy Spirit, you can be confident God is your Abba, your Father. Run into his arms with boldness. Live joyfully, knowing nothing will ever separate you from his love (vv. 38–39). Call on him when you're in trouble, but also call on him when you're not. You don't need an excuse to stay connected to Dad.

Abba, I love you! Thank you for making me your child. Help me to rest in your love.

COMFORT FOR THE JOURNEY

My soul is weary with sorrow;
strengthen me according to your word.

PSALM 119:28

No one escapes this life unscathed. No one sails
through without a storm. We all pick up our share
of scars and sad stories on the journey. For every
mountaintop we experience, this world seems ready to
push us headlong into a jagged valley. It's no wonder
Solomon could examine the human condition from
nearly every angle and conclude, "Everything is
meaningless!" (Ecclesiastes 12:8).

There will be some who want to sugarcoat things,
those who want to push back and say, "It's not all *that*
bad." Truthfully, those folks would be right. We can
find plenty of delight here under the sun. Indeed, God
created a "very good" world (Genesis 1:31). But when
it comes to the happiness we find here, there is a catch:
it's always temporary. Lasting joy, peace, and security
can only come from an eternal source; they can only
come from the Lord.

The Bible contains the very words of God. For
that reason, it's a lifeline to eternity, a letter from home
that reminds us what's true and what really matters to
our Father's heart. Reading Scripture in faith allows us

to taste and savor the freedom and joy we were created for. In the pages of God's Word, we draw near to our Father and discover the riches of his grace. Faint souls are strengthened (Psalm 119:28), minds are renewed (Romans 12:2), and hearts are enlightened (Ephesians 1:18). When this world brings us low, the Word of God can lift us up to the heights of heaven.

Scripture is not a magic pill to swallow or a quick fix for all of life's problems. But ongoing meditation does change a person's trajectory, giving them an eternal perspective. In that, there's tremendous hope and joy. God's Word is a light to dispel shadows, a banner of truth to counter lies, and a healing salve for the nastiest of wounds.

Are you anxious and depressed? Dejected and unable to sleep? Struggling with addiction and feeling trapped? Unable to stand because of the weight on your shoulders? God's Word says, "Cast your cares on the LORD and he will sustain you" (Psalm 55:22). You are not alone. You are loved. You have a future brighter than the stars in the sky. You are unbelievably valuable to the King of creation. And if you ever forget these things, Scripture is waiting to remind you.

God of mercy, be near. Speak to me through your Word.
Lift me up so I can see things as you do.

SPIRIT-LED

"Woe to the obstinate children," declares the LORD, "to those who carry out plans that are not mine, forming an alliance, but not by my Spirit, heaping sin upon sin."

ISAIAH 30:1

Assyria was one of two world superpowers in Isaiah's day. The other was Egypt. So, Israel and Judah, stuck right between the two geographically, often pitted one against the other in an attempt to maintain a fragile peace in the region. On a merely human level, this would seem to be a great strategy. But not when your nation belongs to the Lord of heaven and earth. The nation whose God is the Lord does not need to make alliances with wicked kings in order to survive. The Lord has the strength to keep the peace without making such compromises.

Israel had made a deal with the king of Assyria and became a client state of the empire (2 Kings 16:7–9). There was peace, but it only lasted for a while. Assyria eventually rolled into Samaria with an army and chariots, and decimated the Northern Kingdom (17:3–6). Now, Judah was alone, the remnant of God's chosen nation. But rather than seeing Israel's grievous mistake as a warning, the people looked south to

Egypt, hoping to make a covenant with the nation that once enslaved them and murdered their sons (Exodus 1:8–22).

Listen to what God said to Judah through the prophet Isaiah: "Woe to the obstinate children,…to those who carry out plans that are not mine, forming an alliance, *but not by my Spirit*, heaping sin upon sin" (emphasis added). Forget geopolitics. Forget diplomacy. Judah had one job: to obey Yahweh. It was a sin to act without the direction of the Spirit of God.

Today, many believers live as though the Holy Spirit's direction is an optional feature of the Christian life. They want to tap into the Spirit's guidance when they believe they're all out of options, but barring that level of desperation, they're content to run their own lives.

This is not the way of Jesus, of course. The Spirit isn't a passenger along for the ride as you work things out on your own. God is too good for that. God means for you to be led by the Holy Spirit each and every day (Galatians 5:16). So listen for the voice of Jesus as he speaks through his Spirit inside of you (John 10:4–5), and remember that your life is not your own (1 Corinthians 6:19–20).

Good Shepherd, thank you for not leaving me to stumble through life on my own. I hereby surrender my plans to you.

STARS IN THE NIGHT SKY

Then you will shine among them like stars in the sky as you hold firmly to the word of life.

PHILIPPIANS 2:15–16

Look up on a clear night sometime. Notice what catches your eye first. It's not the darkness of space but the brightness of the stars. The backdrop of blackness only seems to accentuate the light emanating from distant suns. The stars give depth and meaning to the canopy above us; without celestial bodies, there would be nothing to observe, nothing to hold our attention on a warm summer's evening.

In the book of Daniel, we're told that after the resurrection at the end of history, "those who are wise will shine like the brightness of the heavens" (12:3). In the ancient world, people often thought the stars were gods or angels. That's why God forbid his people from worshiping the sun, moon, and stars (Deuteronomy 4:19). While we should never bow a knee to any lesser god, the imagery of angelic stars highlights our destiny. As Daniel revealed, you and I will shine with the righteousness of God for all eternity. We will be made utterly and completely holy, just like those who serve the Lord in the heavenly realm today.

And yet, we need not wait. Paul wrote to the Christians in Philippi to tell them they should "hold firmly to the word of life" (Philippians 2:16)—that is, the gospel. In doing so, he said, they would "shine… like stars in the sky" against the dark background of "a warped and crooked generation" (v. 15). As believers, we're called to live differently than our neighbors who do not know the Lord. By walking according to the truth of God's Word, we will be stars in the night, shining as a beacon to draw men and women out of the darkness.

But here's the incredible thing about stars: they don't have to do anything special to draw attention to themselves. Their light shines simply because of what they are. The more we focus on God instead of ourselves, the more we live out what he has revealed to us in the Scriptures, the brighter we'll shine. As we do, we'll bring glory to him and light the way home for those who are still lost.

Hold on to the gospel. Live your life according to the truth given to you in the Word of God. "Let your light shine before others, that they may see your good deeds and glorify your Father in heaven" (Matthew 5:16). And remember: the darker things get, the brighter your light will be.

Light of the World, forgive me for all the times I have let this world's distractions dim my light. I want to burn brightly for you.

TO BE FILLED AND REFRESHED

Do not get drunk on wine, which leads to
debauchery. Instead, be filled with the Spirit.

EPHESIANS 5:18

When addiction gets hold of a person's soul, it can
be nearly impossible to break free. That's why wine,
beer, and hard liquor can be so dangerous. Men and
women of every background have had their lives
ruined by abusing these drinks. So the question is why
anyone would partake. Just ask a ten-year-old boy who
has snuck a sip of his daddy's beer, and he'll tell you the
taste leaves something to be desired. And then go talk
to someone who has watched a loved one suffer under
the spell of alcoholism; they'll relay horror stories that
will keep you up at night.

With all of its problems, however, alcohol
does do one thing well: it keeps its promises. Getting
drunk is a temporary escape from reality, guaranteed.
In the moment, it feels good. The worries and cares
of this world slip away for a time, and all that's left
is uninhibited bliss. For some, the good time is
just too tempting to pass up. The hangover and the
consequences of an out-of-control evening don't seem
to matter; they crave the short-lived escape. And so,
they keep coming back for more.

God gave us alcohol, and Scripture never forbids our enjoyment of it (except in keeping certain vows; see Numbers 6:1–3). As followers of Jesus, however, we have something better than the sinfulness of getting smashed; we have the Holy Spirit. The apostle Paul actually puts the two experiences side by side, commanding believers not to get drunk while imploring them to be filled with the Holy Spirit.

What's the connection? While alcohol promises an escape from the brokenness and pain of this world, even more so does the Holy Spirit. When we obey the Lord and invite the Holy Spirit to fill us anew, we walk in the joy of the kingdom. We taste the hope we were made for. But more importantly, we have an experience with the living God.

As a Christian, you have received the Holy Spirit, and he's living inside of you right now. But you can be filled by the Spirit again and again. (See Acts 4:31 for an example of believers being "filled with the Holy Spirit" anew.) Draw near to God through prayer and obedience to his Word. Confess your sins and turn from them. Praise the Lord for who he is and what he's done for you. Then ask your Father for a fresh filling of his Spirit. The joy of it will keep you coming back for more.

Everlasting God, I long for a fresh filling of your Spirit. I want more of you in my life.

A WORKER UNASHAMED

Do your best to present yourself to God as one approved, a worker who does not need to be ashamed and who correctly handles the word of truth.

2 TIMOTHY 2:15

Would you buy a kitchen table that isn't level? How about a house that seems to lean to one side? When it comes to construction, we expect clean lines and quality craftsmanship. All things being fair, a carpenter who can't cut straight won't be a carpenter for very long.

When it comes to the way we handle the Word of God, should our standards be any lower? The apostle Paul didn't think so. He told young Timothy to be like "a worker who does not need to be ashamed." He wanted his son in the faith to craft something solid and secure—to study Scripture carefully and faithfully and then teach it to others in a way that honors the Lord. That's what it means to be a person "who correctly handles the word of truth."

Some Bible teachers today barely touch upon the Bible. Their books and messages may contain good advice and lots of spiritual language, but these men and women avoid teaching directly from Scripture as much as possible so as not to offend those who subscribe to the twisted morality of our cultural moment. On the other end of the spectrum are teachers who pride themselves on being orthodox, but all too often, their faithfulness to the text is really just faithfulness to a theological tradition. They teach from the Bible, but they avoid difficult passages. They also dance with all the grace and skill of a ballerina around verses that would seem to invalidate their preconceived positions. Neither type of teacher is being completely faithful to the Scriptures; they're building tables that wobble.

Timothy was a pastor, so Paul directed his instructions toward Timothy's work as a teacher. But that doesn't mean the rest of us are off the hook. We're all ministers. God gave us pastors and teachers to equip us, not to do all the ministry themselves (Ephesians 4:11–12). Besides that, we'll never be able to discern weak or erroneous Bible teaching if we aren't careful students of the Word ourselves.

Spend your life close to Scripture. Read it. Study it. Ask the Holy Spirit to be your guide. When you have questions, dig deeper. When you're unsure about something, be honest enough to admit it. Just keep learning, growing, and building upon what God has shown you.

God who reveals mysteries, lead me into your Word. Correct me when I'm in error. Guide me into truth.

UNFORGIVABLE

"Anyone who speaks a word against the Son of Man will be forgiven, but anyone who speaks against the Holy Spirit will not be forgiven, either in this age or in the age to come."

MATTHEW 12:32

Forgiveness is everything. Without it, we would have no hope of holiness, no hope of eternal life, and no hope of enjoying peace with God. So, when people hear there is a sin that is unforgivable, they sit up and take notice. In fact, the mention of a sin that "will not be forgiven, either in this age or in the age to come" has been the source of countless small group debates and late-night seminary discussions—and who knows how many teenage nightmares.

Jesus said anyone who "blasphemes" (Mark 3:29; Luke 12:10) or "speaks against the Holy Spirit" will be guilty of a sin that cannot be forgiven. At first, that sounds too harsh. Murder, rape, and genocide can all be forgiven, but for some reason, speaking against the Holy Spirit is the lone sin that can't be washed away.

Here is that reason: everything Jesus said and did came as a result of his obedience to the Father (John 5:19) and his reliance upon the Holy Spirit (Luke 4:18–19). Jesus did miracles that testified to his authority through the power of the Spirit. And so, when the Pharisees accused the Lord of performing signs and wonders by the power of the devil (Matthew 12:24), despite plenty of evidence to the contrary, they were endangering their own souls.

Let's be real about what those Pharisees did. A man was possessed by a demon. His life was pure agony. He could neither see nor speak because of the evil that had taken hold of him. And then Jesus changed everything. In the power of the Spirit, he healed the man, restored his sight and voice, and gave him his life back (v. 22). The Pharisees witnessed the scene but, rather than embracing Jesus, concluded, "Nah, that's the devil." It doesn't get much sicker than that!

Every sin can be forgiven—even the initial rejection of Jesus as Lord and Savior—but if people knowingly and continually reject Jesus, to the point where they believe his works are evil, they will have hardened their hearts to the tender mercy of God. They will have pushed away the only Savior there is and will, consequently, remain unforgiven.

Love Jesus. Embrace the power of his Spirit. Test all things (1 John 4:1) but know that God is able to defy every expectation you have.

Spirit of grace, open my heart to all you have for me. Your work in this world is beautiful.

DESERT-ROAD BIBLE STUDY

Philip ran up to the chariot and heard the man reading Isaiah the prophet. "Do you understand what you are reading?" Philip asked.

ACTS 8:30

He was an Ethiopian eunuch. At home, he was used to having a seat at the center of all the action. He was accustomed to giving orders and having others follow them to the letter. Being the finance minister in the queen's court had its advantages. But in Jerusalem, he was an outsider.

When he had arrived at the temple to worship, he was greeted by an imposing sign that forbid him—a foreigner—from going beyond the outer court on penalty of death. Even if he had been native-born, his status as a eunuch would have precluded him from drawing near (Deuteronomy 23:1). He could only get so close to the God he had come to serve.

At the start of his long journey back to Ethiopia, alone in his chariot, the eunuch opened one of the scrolls of the prophet Isaiah and began to read: "To the eunuchs who keep my Sabbaths, who choose what pleases me and hold fast to my covenant—to them I will give within my temple and its walls a memorial and a name better than sons and daughters" (Isaiah 56:4–5).

He was in shock; it was as though the Lord were speaking directly to him.

The Ethiopian began scanning back through the scroll, looking to see what would make such a glorious turnaround possible. And then he found it, and it wasn't a *what* but a *who*: "He was led like a sheep to the slaughter, and as a lamb before its shearer is silent, so he did not open his mouth" (Acts 8:32; compare with Isaiah 53:7).

All this was a prologue to the moment Philip, whom the Holy Spirit had miraculously delivered to that desert road, ran up to the Ethiopian official's chariot and started a conversation. Beginning with that passage in Isaiah, Philip proclaimed the gospel. The rest is biblical history: the Ethiopian responded in faith and was saved, and Philip then baptized him by the side of the road.

Never underestimate the power of studying the Bible with other people. The Lord may have shown things to your brothers and sisters that will help you immensely. At the same time, he has given you much, and you have much to offer. The Holy Spirit knows each of our unique journeys, and so when he brings us together, there's no telling what we'll discover.

Faithful Guide, teach me so that I might teach others. Teach others so that I might learn from them.

MORE PLEASE, LORD

"Let me inherit a double portion of your spirit,"
Elisha replied.

2 KINGS 2:9

There may be no better compliment a child can give
a parent or a protégé can give a mentor than this: "I
love you, and I want to continue your legacy; I want
to follow the Lord just as you have!" That's what Elisha
was really saying to Elijah when he asked for a double
portion of his master's spirit.

If you recall, Elisha was the man the Lord
had chosen to succeed Elijah (1 Kings 19:16), and
Elisha proved to be a willing student. When he was
first called, he gave up the security and wealth of his
parents' farm without so much as a second thought or a
backup plan (vv. 19–21). Later, he clung to Elijah as the
day of his master's departure drew near (2 Kings 2:2, 4,
6). Elisha's request for a double portion does not imply
he wished to be twice as powerful as Elijah. Rather,
it's an echo of the inheritance laws the Lord had given
to ancient Israel. God had commanded every father
to give a double portion of his estate to his oldest son
(Deuteronomy 21:17). That son would then become
the patriarch of the family and assume the position the
father had held in the community.

Elijah's spirit was none other than the Spirit of God. Elisha's request, then, was not only for God to give him Elijah's position as head of the prophets but also for God to continue working through him, just as he had worked through Elijah. He wanted more of the Holy Spirit's power, more of the Spirit's influence over his life, just as Elijah had experienced.

The world today certainly looks different from the way it appeared in Elisha's day, but the desire of his heart should echo within the chest of every kingdom saint just the same. We don't need Elijah as a mentor to want more of the Holy Spirit in our lives. We don't need to be enrolled in the school of the prophets to want more of his presence, his power, and his peace. Honestly, can you think of anything more worthwhile than for God to use you to impact our generation? That's what Elisha was really after—the opportunity to be of greater service to the Lord. And that's what we should be chasing after as well.

Don't settle for the status quo. Ask God to align your heart with his. Open yourself up and invite the Spirit to move through you, to use you to transform this world according to the Father's good purposes.

Immanuel, I want you to live through me. Grant me a double portion of your Spirit.

RAISED ON THE GOOD STUFF

From infancy you have known the Holy Scriptures,
which are able to make you wise for salvation
through faith in Christ Jesus.

2 TIMOTHY 3:15

Kids are amazing. When you think about the amount of information a two-year-old has soaked up in her limited life experience, it's truly mind-boggling. She's learned a language with no formal training, acclimated to the rhythms of her home and family schedule, and sorted out her personal preferences on an ever-expanding number of topics. Along the way, she's also memorized countless storybooks, songs, and nursery rhymes. And while there's still much to learn about our world, the rate at which she's processed new information is truly staggering. No adult has the ability to adjust as quickly.

Most of us can't remember those early years, but what we learned as small children shaped us into the men and women we've become. That was certainly the case with Timothy. He was exposed to the Old Testament from infancy, and it helped to form him into the man of God he became. The Bible has that power, for it reveals God's character and compassion, his holiness and heart. Equipped with that kind of knowledge, a young person is better able to sort out the truth from the lies and is primed to receive the message of salvation.

Given the power of a young child's mind, is there anything more vital to give him than the Word of God? And it's not only children who need the Bible. At every age, what we take in affects how we live. Watch a lot of satirical comedies, and you'll soon find yourself more readily making sarcastic comments. Listen to nihilistic death metal ad nauseam and guess what—you'll quickly feel the burden of hopelessness beginning to weigh you down. Reading the Word of God, however, is like taking a fresh breath of air from the paradise God created you for. It has the power to restore your soul, reset your perspective, and challenge the assumptions the world around you has been feeding you. The more of the Word you take in on a regular basis, the more your heart will beat with the tempo of heaven.

Maybe you grew up in a home where Scripture was a part of everyday life. Or maybe you just started reading the Bible for the first time last month. Either way, the Word of God is for you. You are meant to read it and be transformed by it. Partake. Chew on it. Let it fill you up. There's nothing better for you.

Rabbi Jesus, teach me your ways. May my life become an echo of Scripture.

NO MATTER WHAT COMES

"Now, compelled by the Spirit,
I am going to Jerusalem,
not knowing what will happen to me there."

ACTS 20:22

Paul had plans. He was going to travel to Rome, the most important city in the world. There he would minister to the Christians living under Caesar's shadow, but he would also use the so-called Eternal City as a base of operations for an even greater mission: Paul wanted to go to Spain (Romans 15:24, 28), the final frontier in his day. Jesus had commanded the gospel be preached "to the ends of the earth" (Acts 1:8), and Spain certainly fit the bill.

Before Paul could set out for Rome and Spain, though, he needed to make one other trip first—a short stint to Jerusalem. He needed to deliver an offering he had taken up for believers in need. Paul, as the apostle to the gentiles, knew that Jerusalem could be a dangerous place for him. He had traveled around the empire, declaring that the God of Israel loved people who were not Jews by birth. For such a crime, the religious leaders in Jerusalem wanted Paul dead. But Paul was "compelled by the Spirit" to go (20:22). So he went.

Along the way, he was warned repeatedly that something dreadful would happen to him in Jerusalem. Surprisingly, these warnings came from the Holy Spirit himself (vv. 23; 21:4, 11), the same Spirit who was prodding Paul to continue his journey. Paul understood these warnings did not negate his calling. That's because he knew something critical about the Holy Spirit's operations in this world: the Spirit was not given to us to keep us safe and comfortable; he was given to us so that we might advance the kingdom of God.

The Lord never promised us a life free from suffering. In fact, Jesus seemed to promise we would face trouble as a consequence of aligning our lives with his. The world will hate us for following the Lord (John 15:18–19). And while the Spirit of God may, at times, lead us through this danger and safely out the other side, we have no guarantee of any such thing. At any rate, our goal should be the same as Paul's: to glorify God here on earth, "whether by life or by death" (Philippians 1:20).

Only God knows where your life is headed, so hold it loosely. You belong to him, and he will never let you go. The Spirit is guiding your steps for the sake of the kingdom. Never look back. Just take up your cross and follow (Matthew 16:24). He knows what he's doing.

God who goes before me, I trust you with my life.
Advance your kingdom through me.

THE MERCIFUL WORD

Jonah began by going a day's journey into the city,
proclaiming, "Forty more days
and Nineveh will be overthrown."

JONAH 3:4

While we tend to hold on to God's promises of blessing and favor, times arise when the word of the Lord comes in judgment. It can be downright terrifying. In the days of Jonah the prophet, the people of Nineveh received quite the scare. Jonah marched into town, bleached white from a three-day stint inside the belly of a terrible sea creature, and declared the word God had given him: "Forty more days and Nineveh will be overthrown."

Upon first hearing the pronouncement, it must have seemed rock solid. There was no wiggle room. No conditions. No ultimatum. The message was simple and straight to the point. Forty days would tick on by, and then—*boom!*—the end. No more Nineveh. The Lord of heaven and earth had sent his messenger and, with him, terrible news.

And yet, something in Jonah's message sparked of grace. Why forty days? Why not just destroy the city that weekend? For that matter, why announce the coming judgment at all? If God had already made up his mind, then why give a warning? Jonah could sense God's compassion, even before he set his face toward Assyria. That's what had him running in the wrong direction in the first place (4:2). God gave the people of Nineveh time to respond—to repent and change their evil ways. And they did. To their credit, the Ninevites of that generation embraced the warning from the Lord and turned from their sin. And so, forty days came and went, and God, in his compassion, didn't destroy the city.

God's word goes out to accomplish its purpose (Isaiah 55:11), but sometimes its purpose is to scare us straight: "If at any time I announce that a nation or kingdom is to be uprooted, torn down and destroyed, and if that nation I warned repents of its evil, then I will relent and not inflict on it the disaster I had planned" (Jeremiah 18:7–8).

We're just like the Ninevites. Our sin deserves judgment, not when we die, not forty days from now, but today. And yet God saw fit to stay his hand. And when the judgment came, it came in a way no one could have foreseen: he let it fall upon his Son. "He was crushed for our iniquities; the punishment that brought us peace was on him" (Isaiah 53:5).

Never forget the mercy of God that set you free.

Great Father of mercy, may your warnings of judgment instill within me a hunger for your grace.

JESUS IN YOU

To them God has chosen to make known among the
Gentiles the glorious riches of this mystery,
which is Christ in you, the hope of glory.

COLOSSIANS 1:27

When Luke sat down to pen the second of his two-
volume set, the books we know today as Luke and Acts,
he wrote a few words of introduction to bridge the two
books: "In my former book, Theophilus, I wrote about
all that Jesus began to do and to teach" (Acts 1:1). Did
you catch that? If the gospel of Luke was about all Jesus
"began to do and to teach," then the book of Acts is
about the ongoing work of Jesus.

If you've ever read through Acts, you know that
Jesus ascended to heaven nine verses into the first
chapter. He later appeared to Stephen just before that
faithful soul died a martyr's death (7:55–56), and he
spoke to Saul on the road to Damascus (9:3–6). Other
than those few appearances, though, Jesus is not present
in the book, at least not apparently. But remember,
Luke wants us to see Acts as the continuation of
Jesus' ministry.

The truth is that Jesus is on every page of the
book of Acts. The Holy Spirit was poured out on Jesus'
disciples at Pentecost. In that moment, God came

to dwell with his people. Through the Spirit, Jesus lives within and through every one of us, just as he promised he would: "Anyone who loves me will obey my teaching. My Father will love them, and we will come to them and make our home with them" (John 14:23). That is why, years later, Paul could write to believers in Colossae and tell them the Holy Spirit is "Christ in you, the hope of glory" (Colossians 1:27).

The book of Acts never really ended. Jesus' ministry in this world continues to this day as he works in and through his people. His heart hasn't changed, though. He still wants to see the kingdom come to earth in its fullness, for God's will to be done here "as it is in heaven" (Matthew 6:10). He still wants "to seek and to save the lost" (Luke 19:10). He still wants to heal the broken and afflicted (Matthew 4:23). The only difference is that now he's working through his people.

The Holy Spirit is Jesus in you. Read through the Gospels and consider how he spent his time. Seek out his heart. Learn his rhythms. Give yourself to him and invite him to live through you, wholly and completely. We still have much work to do.

Son of God, I give to you this life you've given me. Make me your hands and feet.

Always in Your Mouth

"Keep this Book of the Law always on your lips; meditate on it day and night, so that you may be careful to do everything written in it. Then you will be prosperous and successful."

Joshua 1:8

In much of the Western world, we are blessed to have options when it comes to the Word of God. We can choose the translation, the format, the cover material, the font size, and whether we want Jesus' words in red. We have access to reference Bibles, reading Bibles, devotional Bibles, and study Bibles galore. And that's just Bibles in print. Don't forget about digital Bibles and audio Bibles.

We are a people awash in the Word of God. Yet, even with all the choices we have, many of us find it difficult to make time to read and study the Scriptures. Could it be that the Bible has become so common that we take it for granted? For most of history, only the wealthy and well-connected had access to the Bible. Ordinary people could not afford their own copy. Perhaps, in that environment, believers were predisposed to understand the Bible's great value and to savor it when they heard it taught. Memorization was the only way for a person to take God's truth with them throughout their days.

When Joshua was commissioned by God to lead the Israelites into the promised land, God told him to keep the Scriptures in his mouth at all times. The Lord wanted his chosen servant to chew on his Word everywhere he went. He wanted him to think about it, meditate on it, breathe it in, and breathe it out. In this way, Joshua would memorize God's commands and be ready to live them out.

In Joshua's day, God's Word only included the first five books of the Bible, and likely, only one copy existed, housed in the tent of meeting. Joshua had access to these scrolls, and God wanted him to lead by example and instruct his people properly. While our situation has certainly changed, God's expectations have not. We have been given access to the holy Word of God, and the Lord wants us to chew on it at all times (Psalm 1:2), to live it out for the world to see (Matthew 5:16), and to instruct others in the ways of the Lord (28:19–20).

God has called you to be a kingdom warrior, and the Word of God is essential to your task. Make sure it's always on your lips so you can take it with you wherever you go.

Lord of all, help me understand your calling on my life. I am your willing servant.

WITH ONE VOICE

The Spirit and the bride say, "Come!" And let the one
who hears say, "Come!" Let the one who is thirsty
come; and let the one who wishes take the free gift
of the water of life.

REVELATION 22:17

The book of Revelation is something of a
rollercoaster. It begins with Jesus dictating letters to
seven first-century churches, but before long we're
dealing with the end of time, and we're awash in beasts
and battles and blood. There's 666 and a dragon and
plagues aplenty. It can be hard to know which way is
up. But then, just as it seems the Bible may be about to
end on a sad note, Jesus enters on a white horse. Eden
is restored. Heaven and earth come together, and God
once again dwells with his people. "He will wipe away
every tear from their eyes, and death shall be no more,
neither shall there be mourning, nor crying, nor pain
anymore, for the former things have passed away"
(21:4 ESV).

It's beautiful. It's everything we've ever longed for.
There on the page are humanity's collective hopes and
dreams described in glorious tones. There will be no
more heartaches and no more disappointments—only
joy and love and the presence of God. And just in case

we missed the implied invitation, the Spirit of God speaks up. Together with the church, Jesus' bride, the Spirit says, "Come!"

It's a small detail, the sort that many readers gloss over, but don't miss it: the Spirit and God's people speak in unison. Their voices are united. In the end, that's what God wants for you: to be in complete sync with his Spirit—to walk in his steps, to speak his thoughts, to be one with the Spirit who is one with the Father and the Son (John 14:15–21).

For too long, too many of us have been trying to figure things out on our own, doing what seems best, even God-honoring. But God has not called us to live as merely good people; he's called us to be *his* people. The only way to do that is to listen to the Spirit's voice. We must pray for discernment to sense his leading. We must open ourselves up to his presence in our lives without reservation. Simply put, we must become one with him. This is the only way to live as God's people in these strange times.

You are a vessel of the Holy Spirit. God lives within you. Once you let that sink in, it will change everything.

Breath of the Almighty, I want everything you have for me. May the world see less of me and more of you.

THE ALL-SUFFICIENT WORD

Jesus did many other things as well. If every one of them were written down, I suppose that even the whole world would not have room for the books that would be written.

JOHN 21:25

The Bible is different from every other book that has ever been written. For starters, the Holy Spirit is its divine author; no other book can claim that. While the human authors and editors of Scripture wrote from their own experience and their own place in history, the Spirit guided them and superintended their work. He also preserved these sacred writings down through the centuries so that what we have today is, in every sense, the Word of God.

The content of the Bible itself is something of a variety pack: sixty-six books written by dozens of authors over a period of more than fifteen hundred years in three different languages. Beyond historical narrative, there are law codes and poems, letters and prophecies, wisdom literature and apocalypse. In addition, the Spirit saw fit to include four separate accounts of Jesus' life, each one providing details the others left out.

Even with all there is to read and study in the Bible, many people wonder if we're missing something.

For starters, some letters of Paul have been lost to history (see 1 Corinthians 5:9; Colossians 4:16), and there are large chunks of Jesus' life and ministry about which we know nothing. Wouldn't it be amazing to be able to fill in some of the gaps?

Actually, no.

The Bible isn't missing anything. The Spirit of God carefully compiled and looked after it to provide us with everything we need for life and faith. Just as every word God speaks is flawless (Proverbs 30:5), so is his written Word.

Many people have said the Bible is a book of answers. In one sense, that's true; the Bible does contain answers to many of our questions. But the Bible isn't an encyclopedia of knowledge. It's not a dictionary to help us label our experiences. It's not a how-to manual either. The Bible is an invitation to know God the Father and Jesus, his Son.

Be encouraged. God knew you before he spoke creation into being (Ephesians 1:4). He knew everything you would face in this life—every trial, every heartache, and every disappointment—and he prepared his Word with you in mind, knowing that one day you would read it.

Nothing's missing. Everything you need is there.

God who draws near, draw near to me. I read your Word not to find answers but to find more of you.

ACKNOWLEDGMENTS

A devotional reading is an odd beast—part illustration, part inspiration, and part Bible study. So while each entry in this book is relatively short, what you see is just the tip of the iceberg. Beneath the surface lay hours of reading, research, reflection, and prayer. I say this as a reminder to myself that while it may be my words that ended up on the page, this book is the product of love and support from family, friends, and colleagues.

My wife, Laurin, is my chief encourager. More times than not, she's the one who creates space for me to write in our busy home. She's also the first person I run to when I stumble upon something new and wonderful about God's plan of redemption. The sweet conversations that result often spill over into my work. So, if you've been encouraged by this devotional, there's a good chance you've been touched by Laurin's good heart.

Speaking of our busy home, every day I am inspired by the three tornadoes God saw fit to bless us with. Jonah, Jude, and Luke, thank you for all the hugs. I love you.

Thanks also to my agent, Teresa Evenson, for helping me to dream big. Finally, I'm grateful to the kind folks at BroadStreet, among them Carlton, Paul, Tim, and Jessica, who championed a simple idea and turned it into this book. It's an honor to partner with you.

ABOUT THE AUTHOR

John Greco is a Bible geek who has spent the bulk of his career futzing with words in the Christian publishing and ministry worlds. He and his wife, Laurin, live just south of Nashville, Tennessee, where they daily wrangle their three boys and dream of someday getting to be the ones who take all the naps. John's website is johngrecowrites.com.